Gan – is that a Polish Name?

For nearly five hundred years
the history
of the Gan family
has been inextricably entwined with that of Poland

Richard L. Gan

Lewis Masonic

First published 2020

ISBN 978 0 85318 590 1

Printed in England

Copyright

Image Credits

Every effort has been made to identify and correctly attribute image credits. Should any error have occurred this is entirely unintentional.

Author: 2,6,7,8,9,10,12,13,14,21,22,23,24,26,27,28,30,31,32,33, 36,37,38,39,43,45,46,50,51,52
Bartov, Omer: 34
Creative Commons, GFDL: 18,40-GralakJ, 41-Mosedschurte, 42-Halibutt, 44,47, 53-Kurowski A, 54-Aung, 55-Anwit,56
Google Maps; 3,4,11,15,35,48,49
Kałamajska-Saeed, M: 5
Public Domain: 1,19,20
Wojskowy Instytut Geograficzny (WIG),1919-1939: 16,17,25,29

Dedication

To my wife Niki
for her patience, encouragement
and support

Acknowledgements

I am grateful for the assistance of Czesław Malewski, the author of *Rodziny Szlacheckie na Litwie w XIX wieku Powiaty Lidzki, Oszmiański i Wileński (Noble families of the Counties of Lida, Ozmiana and Wilno in Lithuania in the 19th century,)*[1] who has provided me copies of three significant documents, held in the Lithuanian State Historical Archives (LVIA): the original deposition confirming the nobility of the Gan family made at the Russian Court of Nobility in Vilna in 1799[2] together with two further court documents dated 1811[3] and 1885[4] respectively which, together with other information he has been able to supply, have been invaluable in helping to build the Gan family-tree back with certainty to 1620, and on the balance of probabilities to 1530.

I have been less than assiduous in my communication with cousins in Poland, usually limited to an exchange of Easter and Christmas cards. The advent of email has certainly made communication that much easier, and 'Google Translate' is of considerable assistance. I am in contact with my second cousins Izabella Pyczel and Robert Gan, the grandchildren of my great-uncle Józef. I am grateful to them both for providing me the details of the family-tree from their side of the family, and in particular to Robert, who was able to obtain archival information regarding my grandfather Franciszek's record as a policeman.

Contents

Illustrations

Preface

In English courts of law there are two standards of burden of proof: *beyond all reasonable doubt* that is - to be certain as to be sure, and the other, *on the balance of probabilities* that is - an occurrence that is more probable than not. These two standards of proof are also a useful tool when it comes to historical research. By and large one can rely on primary sources or documents, such as birth/death certificates, official court records, letters and contemporaneous first-hand accounts in newspapers as being authoritative in providing information that can be accepted as true. Secondary sources, in essence provide second-hand information, that are almost always in published form such as books and articles, and are principally an interpretation of primary sources by a third party not directly involved in the original event. Whilst primary sources are more credible, it is important to use both primary and secondary sources to produce acceptable research.

Introduction

The research of any family history is fraught with difficulties let alone when having to deal not only with the passage of time, but also the complications of records being held in at least five different countries – Poland, Lithuania, Belarus, Russia, and England – together with the difficulty of records being lost as a consequence of successive wars, and not least when attempting to do so a distance of some 1,500 miles, and with only a smattering of Polish.

Family genealogists normally have to rely on church records for details of very old dates of births, marriages and, death and on state records for more recent events.

As far as the Gan family is concerned this presents its own problems as the early church records in question, if they still exist, may be located in Lithuania, Belarus or Poland. However, with the advances that have recently been made in the digitising of records there is already a considerable amount of information that is available and more comes on-line daily.

There is little doubt that access to the internet, and email has made this research possible, but it would have been very much more difficult, if not impossible, were it not for the fact that Gan is one of the oldest noble families of Poland. As a result, it has been possible, using official court records, to trace and document the origin of the family back to at least 1620, when it became a member of the Szlachta - Polish nobility - and granted the right to bear a coat of arms.

Poland ceased to exist as a sovereign state following its third partition in 1795 when, having being divided between Russia, Prussia, and Austria it was finally incorporated as part of the Russian empire. Russia recognised and accepted the nobility of the Polish-Lithuanian Commonwealth as having the same rights, privileges and, status as its own. However, in order to attain and retain that status, it was necessary for an individual member (Szlachcic) of the Polish nobility (Szlachta) to prove their entitlement before specialist courts established for that purpose, and then to continue to register the fact at regular intervals. The first such proof for the Gan family took place in 1799, the record of which is in the Lithuanian State Historical Archives in Vilnius, and the last recorded registration took place in 1885 - a copy of the receipt is retained in the family archive. Given the difficulty in accessing Polish church records, official documents relating to the Szlachta has been a vital source of primary material.

Given the time span involved, almost three hundred years, it is not unexpected that there is a paucity of personal information regarding individual members of the family. Even facts such as dates of birth, marriage, and death are few and far between. One particularly useful source of information has been the geneteka.genealodzy.pl website[5] which has digitised a considerable number of Polish parish records, and very helpfully includes in a small number of instances details regarding the parents of individuals. This has been particularly useful in helping to distinguish between individuals from different generations given the propensity of the Gan family to use a limited number of Christian names, such as Tomasz. In order to provide a complete family tree, in the absence of conclusive information, with respect to dates of birth, death, and marriage certain assumptions have been made regarding the longevity of individuals. The average life-span is taken as sixty years, the age on marriage for men as thirty, and that for women as twenty. When actual dates have subsequently become available and entered on the Family Tree database they have, more often than not, been generally supportive of the original assumption made. Adopting this rationale has resulted in not only identifying gaps that need to be filled but has also enabled the numerous landholdings to be linked with named individual family members.

Introduction

Between the years 1569 and 1819, commencing with the two sons of Andrzej Wasilewicz[6] it is possible through three generations to identify, as shown below, at least twenty-six male siblings and cousins. It is a matter of some regret, and nothing to do with any misogyny on my part, that the females in the family do not feature to any great extent in the official court documents. In the records of births, deaths and marriages, that I have been able to access it is only possible to name and place female members with any degree of certainty where they subsequently appear as a parent at the marriage of an offspring, or where their parents are listed in the few cases of dates of death.

This is probably an appropriate time to declare a personal interest. Whilst the history of all the various branches of the Gan family is of course of importance, what is of particular interest is my own direct descent from Andrzej Wasilewicz, through Piotr Andrzejewicz, shown below.

The complexities involved in a family tree, that runs to fourteen generations are perhaps best illustrated by the fact that in the first three generations of the direct descendants of Andrzej Wasil Gan it has been possible to identify at least twenty-six male siblings and cousins.

With the best will in the world, I have no great wish of taking on the writing of a companion volume to 'War and Peace'. To take on the research of the individual histories of members of the other branches of the family, is a project too far for me. There is plenty of scope and material for others to take on that task with respect to their own branch of the family. I have as far as possible included all known members of the Gan family in the definitive Family Tree, and at the conclusion of this history produced a further extract that stems from my paternal grandfather Franciszek Ludwik, but I am also acutely aware that there is more work that warrants to be done. Indeed, this whole project and book should be considered nothing more than 'a work in progress'.

Gan – is that a Polish Name?

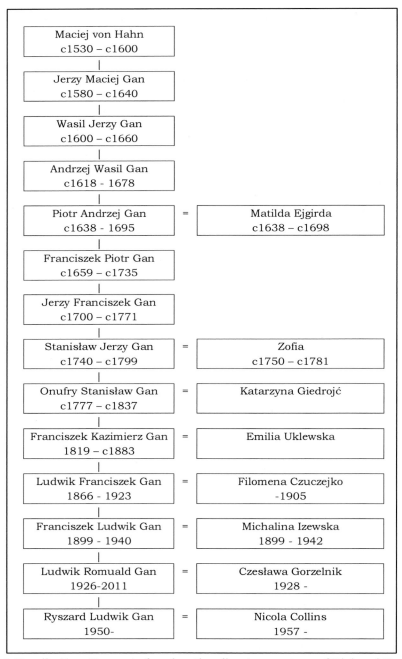

1 Family Tree Excerpt showing the direct ancestors of Richard Gan

Introduction

A family history should be more than just the production of a family tree, although it is undoubtedly one important element, and for it to be of any interest or value it should also attempt to be a social history. At the time of writing the family tree contains in excess of 650 names, to print it would require twenty pages of A4, or one sheet of paper some three metres by two metres in size. Accordingly, for the sake of clarity a number of extracts from the family tree are included in the body of the text. A more detailed extract, running to some eight pages is included as an annex, as is an index of all known family members with the surname Gan, together with a further index of those known female members of the family who changed their surname on marriage.

Before embarking on the detailed history of the Gan family there are a number of factors that need to be drawn to the attention of the reader, together with some information, that hopefully will clarify and provide some context to those who may not familiar with aspects of Polish history.

These include the conundrum of the Polish-Lithuanian Commonwealth and whether the family could in fact be considered to be Lithuanian rather than Polish. The significance of the Szlachta or Polish Nobility whose characteristics are unique in western Europe. The rights, privileges, and obligations that were granted to a Szlachcic. The benefits that accrued to the family for a period of over three-hundred years as a consequence of being members of the Szlachta. The system of Polish Heraldry, again almost completely different to that elsewhere in western Europe and inextricably linked with the Szlachta.

Context

The situation regarding the long history of the Polish-Lithuanian Commonwealth is complex to say the least. At one time or another it will have had, living within its territorial boundaries, a population consisting of a considerable number of different ethnic groups. The 1897 Russian census, for what is now Lithuania, gave a population of about 2.7 million broken down as follows: 60% Lithuanians; 15% Belarusian, Russian, and Ukrainian; 13% Jewish; and 15% Polish, of whom 9% were Szlachcic (i.e. a member of the Szlachta).[7] A graphic illustration is that the capital, was known by the various groups as: Wilno: Polish; Vilnius: Lithuanian; Vilne: Yiddish; Vil'nius: Russian; Vil'nia: Belarussian; and Wilna: German. The area where the Gan family became established was in the north-east part of the Commonwealth, in the former Grand Duchy of Lithuania. Prior to the Second World War, notwithstanding the ethnic breakdown the language spoken in a third of homes was Yiddish; the day to day language, of officialdom, business, church, and school was Polish; whilst the language in rural areas, where 87% of the population lived, was largely Belarussian. At the outbreak of the War, in 1939, there was almost no Lithuanian spoken in Vilnius.[8]

The question needs to be asked is the Gan family Polish or Lithuanian? In a territorial and national sense, it should undoubtedly be considered Lithuanian, but in terms of cultural identity, even though living in Lithuania for many generations, the Gan family, has always considered itself to be Polish. Something it shares with many other families in similar circumstances, with perhaps one of the most notable examples being that of Adam Mickiewicz, considered to be Poland's greatest poet whose family estate at Zaosie was only forty miles from the Gan's estate, Folwark[9] Han at Ruda Jaworska.

Membership of the aristocracy or nobility in England is estimated to be somewhat less than 2% of the total population. In Poland, the figure was something in excess of 10%, or some

60,000 families.[10] In addition, unlike most of Europe, there were no aristocratic titles within the Szlachta.[11] By the 16th century membership of the Szlachta could only be secured in one of three ways: by being born into a noble family, adopted in heraldic terms by a noble family,[12] or ennobled by the king[13] or the Sejm (Polish Parliament); prior to that nobility could be achieved by the acquisition of land, and the acknowledgment by one's neighbours.

With the passage of time, through legislation combined with custom and practice; the Szlachta derived a number of very important rights and privileges.[14] These included the participation in the election of the Kings of the Polish-Lithuanian Commonwealth; an entitlement for the family to be granted a coat of arms, and at the other end of the scale exemption from corporal punishment, and shackling during a criminal investigation. However, one downside was that a szlachcic was forbidden to engage in trade or commerce, under the penalty of the loss of their noble status.[15]

It has been argued that szlachta is a form of caste system rather than a social classification in the same mould as the Kshatriyas of India and the Samurai of Japan. The concept of 'face' was important to a szlachcic and its association with dignity, prestige, and status in terms of their social relationships. One of its manifestations was that of dress. No matter how impoverished a szlachcic would always endeavour to keep up appearances with his neighbours.

The prescribed dress for a szlachcic well into the 18th century included a scimitar-like szabla - sabre when outdoors, and a dagger indoors, thigh-length boots, a żupan[16] worn under a kontusz,[17] bound with a pas kontuszowy.[18]

In theory all members of the Szlachta were considered to be equal in status, but with the passage of time it was inevitable that some form of differentiation would evolve. It is possible to identify and distinguish at least eight different categories,[19] including one that became known as the Średnia szlachta or folwarczna szlachta - middle nobility. These were the possessors of one or more village or estate, as well as owning a small number of serfs. The group comprised some 40% of all Polish nobility, and included the Gan family.

The occupation by Russia following the first partition of Poland in 1772 resulted in members of Polish nobility being required to prove their pedigree before a district court. In 1785 Empress Catherine II ordered the preparation of separate and distinct genealogical archives for the nobility in all provinces of the Empire. Six categories of nobility were recognised, the largest being that of the ancient noblesse - old aristocracy, noble families from before 1685, comprising some 2,681 families, or about 39% of the total.

The importance of being a Szlachcic and the privileges it attracted cannot be overstated. Families were required to provide the Court with detailed documentation and genealogies, in order to prove entitlement to noble status. The requirements did not affect the Gan family until after the third partition of Poland in 1795, and the Russian occupation of the Województwo [Voivodeship – Province] of Wilno and Powiat [County] of Oszmiana. The family appeared before the court in Wilno on 8 February 1799, when it was able to prove its status as ancient noblesse, and were issued with a decree confirming their nobility and the right to bear a coat of arms.

The Szlachta is believed to have its genesis from the *ród* or clan, a lineage structure that can be traced back to the first half of the 11th century. The origins of the Polish heraldic system - *herbarz* - is based on the *ród* which adopted a coat of arms as a means of easy recognition in battle, so as to help distinguish friend from foe, in addition each coat-of-arms has its own name, usually, the ancient rallying or war-cry or the name of the ród. Whereas in most European heraldry the object was to identify an individual, in Poland all the members of a Ród, used the same undifferenced arms.

2 Szlachic Polski – Polish Nobleman by Jan Piotr Norblin 1817

Context

Admission to a ród was based on patronage. A prominent land owner could act on his own initiative, and invite friends and relations into his clan. However, the most prominent patron was the king who could use his prerogative - *Nobilitacja* - the royal grant of ennoblement – to assign individuals to a clan of his choice thereby enabling them to share in all privileges of the szlachta, and entitle them to bear the coat of arms of that particular clan, which is what happened to the Gan family in 1620, when they were admitted into the Rawicz ród.

One significant effect of this unique arrangement was that it became customary to refer to a nobleman by both his family name and his coat of arms - hence Gan *herbu* Rawicz, the equivalent of 'de' in French and 'von' in German.

In some instances, families have taken the opportunity to hyphenate the two elements to form a double-barrelled name, such as Rawicz-Gan, but that is not something that the Gan family found necessary. Having stated that my great-great-grandfather, Franciszek (1819-c1883), for reasons that are explained later did for a time refer to himself as Gieysztor-Gan.

The Rawicz Clan, whose battle cry was Rawa, is mentioned as early as 1334.[20] The coat of arms that the Gan family are entitled to bear is shown on page 20. The translation of the blazon[21] as described by Niesiecki in his *Herbarz Polski*[22] of 1841 which is a little more elaborate than the depiction used in English heraldry[23]:

> *The girl should have flowing hair, wearing a crown on her head, both arms extended up and slightly raised, in a dress covering her shoulders with bare arms, sitting on a black bear, facing left, right front leg raised as if running on a yellow background. On a helmet above the crown between two deer horns, the top half of a bear, turned to the left side[24], as if sitting, front left leg lowered, holding a rose in his right raised leg.*

The legend behind the derivation of the blazon can be found in Szymon Okolski's encyclopaedia of the Polish nobility *Orbis Polonus* of 1643.[25] It concerns the actions of Sweyn, who was charged with providing a dowry for his cousin Clotilda, following the death of his father, King Knut the Great (Canute) of England.[26] An alternative version of the legend is that a princess is sealed, by her brothers, in a cave overnight, where it is known that a bear has its lair, so that on her death her brothers may inherit her fortune. The next day when the stone blocking the entrance of the cave is rolled back the princess rides out unharmed on the back of the bear. The princess lives happily ever after, and the brothers are dealt with accordingly.

The moral behind the legend is that not only good triumphs over evil, but also that the virtuous and innocent can overcome and even tame the innate brutality inherent in wild creatures.

The absence of a Polish college of heralds resulted in a complete lack of control over coats of arms. One consequence is that over time different versions - *odmiany* – of a coat of arms would materialise usually using different colours. However, any such variations they are still considered to be the same coat of arms.

The heraldic expert, Juliusz Ostrowski, has identified some thirty different variations in those of individual families entitled to the Rawicz coats of arms;[27] including: the arrangement of the hands of the princess, her position in relation to the bear, the addition of a crown, changes in the colour of the background, the bear holding a red rose - white rose - or no rose at all, and the bear with his tongue in – or - out.
The most common arrangement was for the princess to be sitting on the back of a bear, and although Niesiecki did not specify the colour of the dress, the most commonly depicted is red. Give that some 460 families are entitled to use the Rawicz coat of arms, it is perhaps surprising that the number of variations is not even greater. Insofar as the Gan coat of arms are concerned the variations include: a purple dress, the bear

holding a red rose, with his tongue in, and more significantly facing the opposite direction to that depicted on the shield.

The rule of primogeniture does not apply in Poland so by custom and practice all legitimate children of a nobleman, both male and female, could inherit their father's coat of arms – that is the coat of arms of his clan - without any differentiation, together with all his privileges as a noble. This partly accounts for the relatively large proportion of Polish families entitled to a coat of arms by the 18th century.

The privileges of the Szlachta including the usage of arms were abolished in 1921, by the first Constitution of the Polish Republic,[28] but this particular article was rescinded in the Constitution of 1935 – Article 81(ii), in practical terms, this was of little or no consequence, not least because of the outcome of the Second World War.

Mercenaries

1530 – 1658

It is probable that our Polish family name of Gan originates from a noble German family named Hahn also known as Von Han. It is known that one member of that branch of that family journeyed to the Duchy of Courland, then a fiefdom of Poland, where in 1561 he was ennobled by Zygmunt II August King of Poland.[29] It is not unreasonable to presume that this may have been for services rendered to the king as a mercenary. There are a number of recorded military engagements in both Courland[30] and Livonia[31] in the period 1557 to 1583,[32] that would have given an enterprising and adventurous soldier the opportunity of finding military action.

Some sixty years later, in July 1620 the family having already been ennobled in the Court of Nobility of the Duchy of Courland, King Zygmunt III, conferred on Jerzy Maciejowicz Gan, membership of the hereditary Szlachta of Polish-Lithuania, admission to the Rawicz clan, the right to bear a coat of arms, together with the ownership of Folwark Nemowiany, a manor house in Oszmiana.[33]

In 1578 the Sejm deprived the king of his power to create new grants of ennoblement [34], other than for outstanding bravery on the battlefield so an assumption can be made that his elevation was a reward for his courage in the service of the king in one of the many battles that took place between 1817 and 1821.[35]

It was not unusual in Poland, as in Russia, for names to include the patronymic,[36] hence it is entirely feasible given the time-line, that Maciej von Han, the father of Jerzy Maciejowicz von Han, was the son of the man who had been ennobled in 1561 in the Duchy of Courland by King Zygmunt II August, some 350 miles north of Oszmiana.

3 The Gan Family Coat of Arms

Maciej 〉 **Jerzy** 〉 **Wasil** 〉 **Andrzej** 〉 Piotr 〉 Franciszek 〉 Jerzy 〉

The first map below shows the position in 1648 of the Polish-Lithuanian Commonwealth - the largest country in western Europe at the time, and the second map the path of the journey likely to have been undertaken members of the von Han family, to the Powiat of Oszmiana in 1772.

4 Map showing the extent of the Polish-Lithuanian Commonwealth in 1648

There are a number of pieces of evidence that confirm the nobility of the Gan family and their establishment in Oszmiana, this includes the fact that Anna-Małgorzata, the

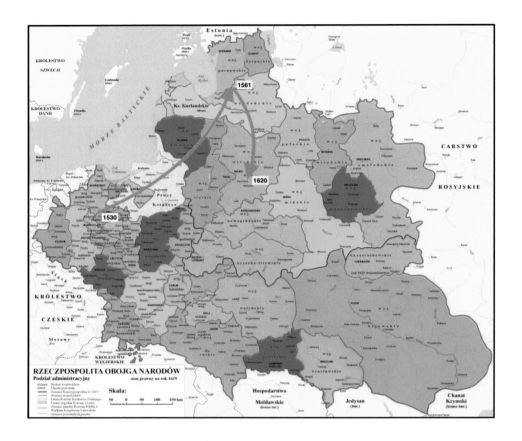

5 Probable Route taken by Von Han from Prussia to Oszmiana

daughter of Jerzy von Han, married Jan-Krzysztof Neuhof von der Ley, a member of the German noble family and heir to Datnental estates, who died in 1710.[37]

The significance is twofold, as it not only gives support to the German family connection, but also the fact that marriage between members of the nobility was restricted to those who were able to prove their noble descent for three generations on both the paternal and maternal side.

Maciej ⟩ **Jerzy** ⟩ **Wasil** ⟩ **Andrzej** ⟩ Piotr ⟩ Franciszek ⟩ Jerzy ⟩

6 The Powiat of Oszmiana - 1772

When Andrzej Wasilewicz, was named as the heir to the estates of Zarojście in Oszmiana, and granted the right to own land in June 1650 he was acknowledged as belonging to one of the long standing and ancient families in the Kingdom of Poland and Lithuania, and it is from him that our branch originates.[38]

The German origin of the family is further alluded to when it is described as "...one of the well-known and established noble families of Courland who subsequently married into other noble families, such as the German Neuhof von der Ley, and of greater significance the noble Polish family of Ejgird in Oszmiana."[39]

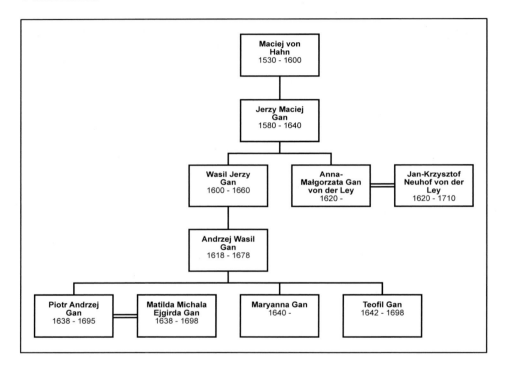

7 Family Tree Excerpt showing the earliest origins of the family

The marriage referred to above is that of Piotr Andrzeiewiecz, son of Andrzej Wasilewicz who on his marriage to Matilda Ejgird in February 1658, received a dowry from her father Jan Czyczyn Ejgird of part of the villages of Ejgirda and Sieliszczena in the Powiat of Oszmiana. This event is well documented in a number of different sources, including that of the Ejgird family.[40]

Maciej 〉 **Jerzy** 〉 **Wasil** 〉 **Andrzej** 〉 Piotr 〉 Franciszek 〉 Jerzy 〉

The transformation from von Han to Gan merits some explanation. The reason for Gan rather than Han is relatively straight forward and a direct consequence of the Russian occupation of Polish-Lithuanian Commonwealth in 1795. For the first time it became necessary for individual members of the nobility to prove their entitlement before specialist courts established for that purpose. There being no equivalent to the letter 'H' in the Russian alphabet, government officials appear to have made a unilateral decision and taken the easiest of options in translating the Polish 'H' into a Russian 'G' – it being the next letter in the alphabet, and thus at a stroke of a pen the family Han became the family Gan.

It is not clear when the Polish version of Han was adopted or the Germanic noble designation of 'von' was dropped.[41] For the sake of clarity, with the exception of Maciej von Hahn, the name Gan is used throughout on the basis that the earliest formal documentation refers to Jerzy Maciej Gan, notwithstanding the fact that the name Han would have been used until 1795.

The early history of the family from 1530 to 1658 is one of the foundation of a family dynasty, carefully arranged marriages, the acquisition of property, and the establishment of the family as major landowners in the district of Oszmiana.

The deposition confirming the nobility of the Gan family made at the Russian Court of Nobility in Vilna in 1799, referred to above, makes it possible to piece together not only family relationships but also land holdings.

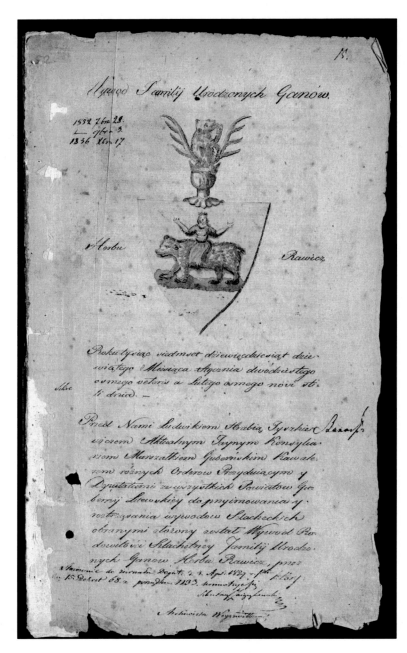

8 Official Court Document of 1799
establishing the nobility of the Gan Family

Maciej ⟩ **Jerzy** ⟩ **Wasil** ⟩ **Andrzej** ⟩ Piotr ⟩ Franciszek ⟩ Jerzy ⟩

The first page of the eleven-page document, which is held in the Lithuanian State Historical Archives [42], illustrated above is headed with the Rawicz coat of arms (note that the bear in the crest is facing sinister), and translated as follows:

> *Genealogy of the Family Born with the name Gan held on 28 January, old calendar (Julian), 8 February, new calendar (Gregorian) 1799.*

> *'Before us, Count Ludwik Tyszkierwi Banarpo, the current Consul Marshal for the Government of Knights and various noble Orders. Deputised to hear matters concerning admission, and disputes relating to the Szlachta in all the Districts within the Governorship of Lithuania. An interview was held with the noble family born with the name of Gan and the coat of arms of Rawicz, (continues on page 2) ...who proved that the family were from the most ancient times hereditary members of the Szlachta in the Powiat of Oszmiana and owned estates granted as a privilege to Jerzy Maciej Gan by Zygmunt King of Poland on 15 July, in the year 1620...'*

The document is annotated with further dates 1832 and 1836 at the top of page 1, and 1829 at the bottom, which indicates that further submission and updates were made periodically. The document details the genealogy of the various branches of the family and confirmation of their membership of the szlachta, together with information regarding their property holdings.

Andrzej Wasilewicz, is acknowledged as the forebear of the two main branches of the present-day Gan family through his two sons Piotr Andrzejewicz, and Teofil Andrzejewicz, who in turn had seven sons, and three sons respectively.

Gan – is that a Polish name?

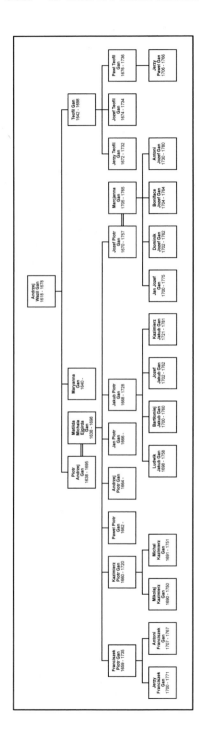

9 Family Tree Excerpt showing the line from Andrzej Wasil Gan to Jerzy Franciszek

Landowners

1658 – 1800

The period in question is very fallow in terms of any personal information regarding specific individuals. We have their names, some information regarding significant dates such as birth, death and marriage, which together with information derived from documents such as the 1799 Genealogical Court deposition enables relationships and a family tree to be drawn up. Most significantly the latter enables details regarding the property holdings, held by various members of the family, to be catalogued in some instances, up to as late as 1939, including: villages, estates, land, individual houses, and in a small number of cases even - serfs.

The property holdings, have been collated into the form of a table, that lists the names of the property together with details of the individual owners, and the date(s) of ownership.[43] All the properties in question were originally in Polish-Lithuania and with a few exceptions entirely in the Powiat of Oszmiana, but which today would be situated in what became Belarus in 1945. In each case the original Polish spelling is given with the current Belarus equivalent, together with their geographical coordinates, which enables them to be located on present-day maps.

Whilst there are undoubtedly others that are yet to be confirmed, to date twenty-two properties have been positively identified as having belonged to members of the family. These are displayed on the accompanying modern-day map, the numbering corresponding with that in the table. All but four are in the Powiat of Oszmiana and take the form of a 'ribbon-development' along what is now the P48 road stretching from Oszmiana in the north, through Holszany and Traby, to Juraciszki in the south,[44] a distance of some 30 miles. The range of properties include villages, granges, manors, backwaters, a town house, a clay deposit and a forest. The four properties that are situated beyond the Oszmiana-Juraciszki line are the three original estates of Folwark Nemowiany, Zarojście, and Hurajnowszczyzną; and from the point of view of this branch of the family, the last family owned estate of Folwark Han, in the neighbouring Województwo of Nowogródek.

As previously stated Folwark Nemowiany was granted by King Zygmunt III to Jerzy Maciejowicz in 1620. I have not been able to find any trace of a place called Nemowiany, or anything approximating to it. However, the ownership of Folwark Nemowiany passed from Jerzy Maciejowicz, to his son, Wasil and thence to his son to Andrzej Wasilewicz. The document of 1799 refers to the family's hereditary estate of Wasilewszczyzna. It seems entirely reasonable to speculate that the original property of Nemowiany was renamed by its second owner Wasil.

In addition to inheriting the Wasilewszczyzna estate, Andrzej Wasilewicz also acquired, possibly as part of a dowry, an estate in Zarojście, and subsequently bought from Alexi Zyburowicz Hurynowicz, in June 1650, the village of Hurajnowszczyzną.

Piotr Andrzeiewiecz had seven sons, including Franciszek Piotrowicz from which our branch of the family is descended. He appears to have been the eldest, as on the death of his father in 1695 he inherited half the Ejgird estate, the other half being shared between the other six brothers.

Franciszek Piotrowicz in his will of 1735 left the Ejgird estate to his eldest son Jerzy Franciszek, whilst the estate at Seliszczenięta went to his other son Antoni Franciszek, which in turn passed to his son Stanisław Antoni in 1792.

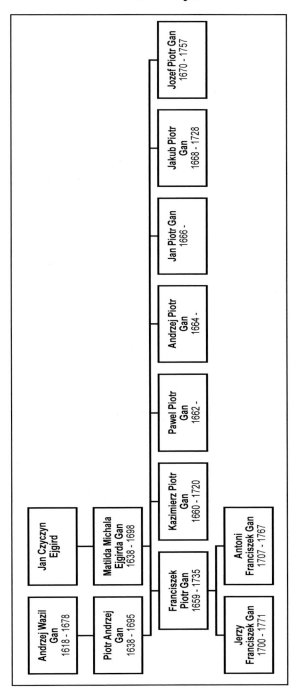

10 Family Tree Excerpt showing Piotr Andrzej and his seven sons

Gan – is that a Polish name?

11 Table of Estates, Villages, and Land held by the Gan Family 1620 to 1939

	From To	Estate, Village, Land Holding	First Known Owner	Last Known Owner	Current Location	Geographic Coordinates
1	1620	Folwark Nemowiany Wasilewszczyzna [31]	Jerzy-Maciej Gan Wasil-Jerzy		Vasilevshchina	53.777417, 27.351304
2	1650	Zarojście Malinowszczyzna	Andrzej-Wasilc c1618-c1678		Malinowshchyna	54.330082, 26.656230
3	1650	Hurajnowszczyzną [32]	Andrzej-Wasilc c1618-c1678		Gurnovshchina	53.053333, 26.750000
4	1658 1855	Ejgirdowszczyzna Ejgirdy [33]	Piotr-Andrzej c1638-c1695	Tomasz 1775-1864 [34]	Eigerdy	54.061800, 26.065512
5	1658 1850	Seliszczenięta[35]	Piotr-Andrzej c1638-c1695	Bartłomiej c1817-c1902[36]	Selishchenyata	54.066151, 26.044491
6	1817	Folwark Garlinszczyzna	Józef c1799-c1855 [37]		Garlinshchina	54.472537, 26.086075
7	1850 1850	Zaścianek Małe Ejgirdy	Tomasz 1775-1864	Bartłomiej c1817-c1902 [38]	Ejgirdy	54.066156, 26.062255
8	1835	Dwor Dorże	Józef c1799-c1855		Dorzhi	54.263104, 25.832779
9	1795	Okolica Czyczynowszczyzna	Tomasz 1775-1864		Eigerdy	54.061800, 26.065512
10	1795 1855	Miasto Juraciszki	Tomasz 1775-1864	Jerzy c1851-c1911[39]	Juraciški	54.032373, 25.926584
11	1818	Łejłubka	Tomasz 1775-1864		Leilubka	54.444117, 25.962453
12	1821 1825	Prackowszczyzna	Tomasz 1775-1864		Pratskovshchina	54.486401, 25.988875
13	1828	Bohdaniszki	Tomasz 1775-1864		Bogdanishki	54.420597, 25.981962
14	1874	Zaścianek Szczuczy Bór	Tomasz 1775-1864		Szczuczyn	53.607867, 24.738691
15	1840	Morgi, Oszmiana	Tomasz 1775-1864		Ashmany	54.420110, 25.940081
16	1798 1844	Wieś Kozłowszczyzna	Tomasz 1775-1864		Kozlovshchina	54.212903, 25.965814
17	1813 1850	Dorgiszki	Tomasz 1775-1864		Dorgishki	54.219128, 25.959639
18	1813 1902	Paszkiszki	Tomasz 1775-1864 [40]	Juliusz c1867-c1927 [41]	Pashkishki	54.217177, 25.929345
19	1823	Okolica Kamionka	Gan - No further information		Kamenka	54.306914, 25.977749
20	1843	Rodziewicze	Gan - No further information		Rodzyevichy	53.965289, 25.885136
21	1843	Santoka	Gan - No further information		Santaka	54.409340, 23.245000
22	1883 1939	Folwark Han Ruda Jaworska	Franciszek Kazimierz Gan 1819-c1883	Feliks, Józef, Franciszek	Ruda Yavorskaya	53.410800, 25.158300

Glossary: Folwark [Grange]; Zaścianek [Backwater]; Dwór [Manor House]; Okolica [Area]; Miasto [Town]; Bór [Forest]; Wieś [Village]

Landowners

Andrzej 〉 **Piotr** 〉 **Franciszek** 〉 **Jerzy** 〉 **Stanisław** 〉 **Onufry**〉

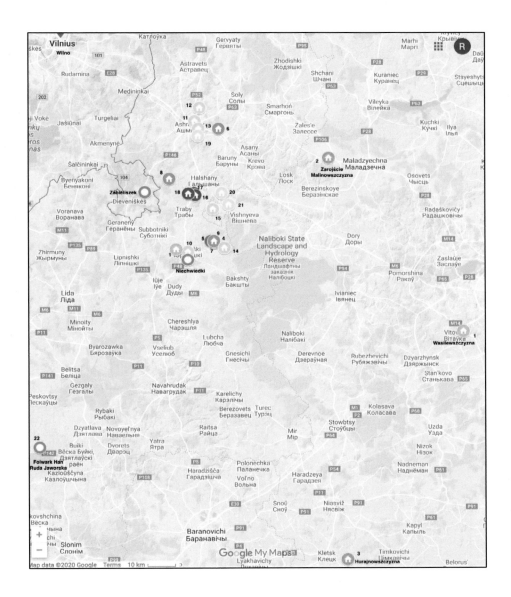

*12 Map showing Estates, Villages, and Land held by the Gan Family
1620 to 1939*

The estates of Ejgirdy, Seliszczenięta, Małe Ejgirdy, and Czyczynowszczyzna can be shown to have remained within the family as late as 1902, but with the passage of time there appears to have been considerable movement of properties between the various branches of the family. Ejgirdy and Seliszczenięta passed from the line of Franciszek Piotrowicz to his brother Kazimierz Piotrowicz. The early involvement of the family in civic matters is highlighted by the fact that Kazimierz Piotrowicz, exercised his right to cast his vote in favour of Augustus II, the Strong, as King of Poland in the election of 1697;[45] following in the footsteps of his father Piotr who is recorded as having voted for King Jan III, Sobieski in 1674.[46]

Ejgirdy and Seliszczenięta were in due course inherited by Tomasz Marcin (1775-1864), the great-grandson of Kazimierz Piotrowicz, who also became the owner of Małe Ejgirdy, and Czyczynowszczyzna, and who as the table shows was a major landowner in the area, with at least eleven properties to his name. The family's involvement in civic affairs is demonstrated by the fact that in 1843 Tomasz Marcin is listed as a Boundary Judge.[47] His grandson Jerzy (c1851-c1911) is listed in 1885 as one of the 104 major landowners in Polish-Lithuania with some 434 dziesięcina[48] or 1,169 acres (473 hectares) to his name. Whilst Jerzy's father Mikołaj, served as a Boundary Judge in the Powiat of Oszmiana between 1830 and 1840, and in 1859 is listed as a Deputy in the Forestry Commission.

Seliszczenięta meanwhile reappears back in the ownership of the Antoni Franciszek line of the family, when in about 1850 it is shown to be in the ownership of his great-grandson Bartłomiej (c1817-c1902), who is also shown as the owner Małe Ejgirdy previously owned by his third cousin Tomasz Marcin.

The family relationships are shown below in the two extracts from the definitive family tree. The properties cited above are all in relatively close proximity as highlighted on the map below dating from 1927.

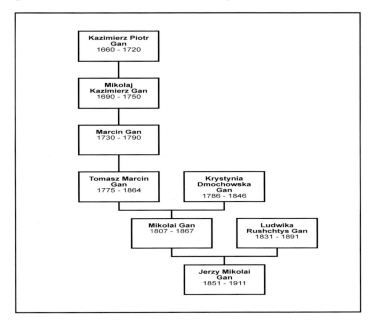

*13 Family Tree Excerpt showing the Kazimierz Piotr Gan
branch (brother of Franciszek Piotr)*

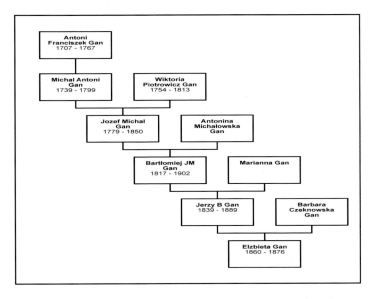

*14 Family Tree Excerpt showing the Antoni Franciszek Gan
branch (younger son of Franciszek Piotr)*

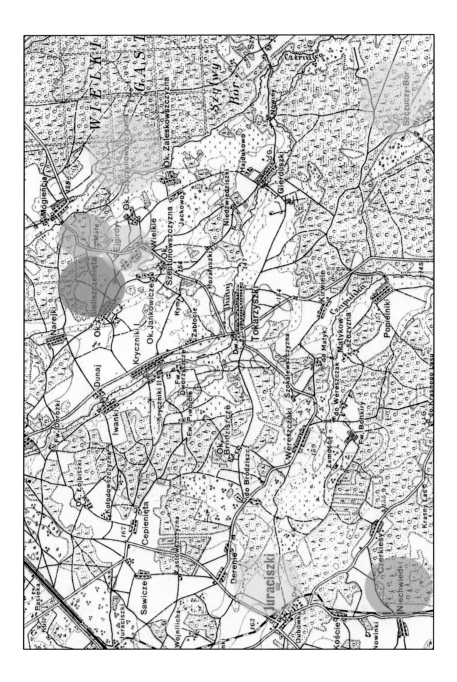

15 Map showing properties owned by the Gan family in and around Edgirdy

Landowners

Andrzej ⟩ **Piotr** ⟩ **Franciszek** ⟩ **Jerzy** ⟩ **Stanisław** ⟩ **Onufry**⟩

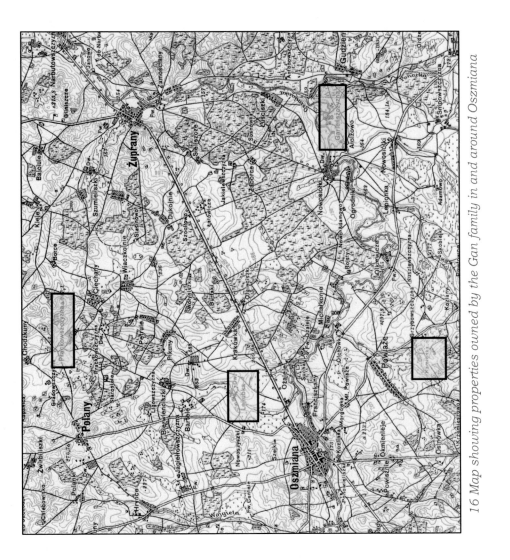

16 Map showing properties owned by the Gan family in and around Oszmiana

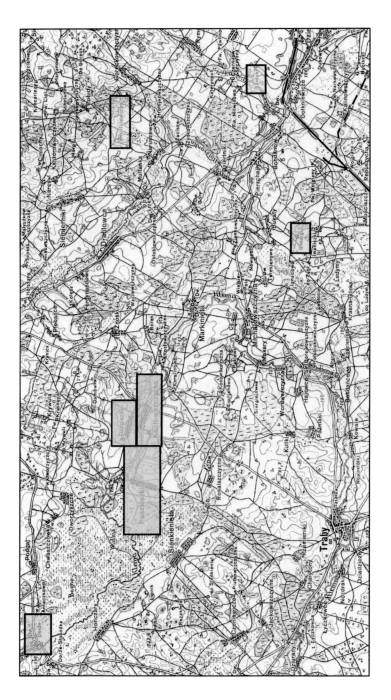

17 Map showing properties owned by the Gan family in and around Traby

Andrzej 〉 **Piotr** 〉 **Franciszek** 〉 **Jerzy** 〉 **Stanisław** 〉 **Onufry**〉

The relationship between the two families Gan and Ejgird first linked by marriage in 1658, continued for over 180 years. There are recorded a number of marriages between members of the two families:

	Gan	**Ejgird**
1658	Piotr	Matilda
1789	Michał	Klofa
1795	Anna	Rafał
1798	Bartłomiej	Barbara
1812	Stefan	Marianna
1826	Marianna	Józef
1842	Kazimierz	Zuzanna

This may be taken as an indication that neither family moved very far from its original roots. It is a phenomenon that can be found in rural areas throughout the world including England, where the distance one travelled to find a suitable marriage partner was most likely determined either by how far one could walk, or further afield if wealthy enough to own a horse or cart. Analysis of census returns in England has shown that until 1851 about 40% of couples met and married within 3 miles of their birthplace. [49]

The table of properties above highlights some interesting issues that are not possible to answer without further research and access to records such as census returns. There is a geological maxim to the effect that geological events taking place in the world today will also be found to have taken place in the historical past. Thus, for example, we know that at the turn of 19th century Ludwik Franciszek had four sons, and three daughters all of whom were living, and at one time working on the estate at Ruda Jaworska. The same would have applied in preceding generations. Whilst it has been possible to identify a number of the properties owned by the Gan family it is not yet been possible to determine exactly who was actually living in them at any one time. We know, for example that Piotr Andrzej had seven sons, and whilst we know a little about Franciszek Piotr, and Kazimierz Piotr, nothing has yet come to light about the other five sons, their extended families or where exactly they lived. The main principle lying behind the ownership of any estate would have been one of self-sufficiency. As such the main activities would have been farming, the management of the land, the estate and all the various associated support activities. There is little doubt that as far as labour around the farm or estate was concerned if would have been fulfilled to some lesser or greater extent by the use of serfs.

In 1850 Tomasz Marcin Gan is shown as the owner of the Paszkiszki estate, the manor house and village had been offered for sale in 1800 by Tadeusz Zakrzewski for PLN 56,000.[50] The whole estate comprised of two villages and some 892 dziesięcina, or 2,400 acres (972 hectares); in the village of Paszkiszki itself there were listed four serfs: Dzieniesienko, Gajduczenko,[51] Jakowczyk, and Wierzbołowicz; and in the village of Dorgiszki, a further four serfs: Augustynowicz, Dzieniesienko, Gajduczenko, Trzaskowski together their respective dependents comprising sixty-five males and fifty-seven females.[52]

The first step towards the abolition of serfdom in Poland was taken in the Constitution of May 1791, and although full abolishment was enacted by the Proclamation of Połaniec in 1794, both initiatives were overtaken by the third and final partition of Poland in 1795. Serfdom was abolished in Prussia in 1807, Austria in 1848, but not until 1861 in Russia and hence Lithuanian-Poland. In 1778 Serfs made up some 75% of the population in Poland compared with 10% szlachta, and 15% town dwellers or burghers.[53] John-Jacques Rousseau was quite scathing in his assessment that "...the Polish nation is composed of three orders: the nobles, who are everything; the burghers, who are nothing; and the peasants, who are less than nothing".[54] Although serfdom may have been officially abolished, it did not disappear entirely but rather was transformed into a system of indentured-labour, continuing

Andrzej 〉 **Piotr** 〉 **Franciszek** 〉 **Jerzy** 〉 **Stanisław** 〉 **Onufry**〉

much as before save that in theory, individuals were not tied to any one particular employer and were paid for their work.

The issue of not being able to identify which individual members of the family were resident in any one particular property is of some significance for our own branch. It is known, for example, that Piotr Andrzej, Franciszek Piotr, and Jerzy Franciszek were owners of Ejgird, and we also know that their successors will also have been landowners, else they would not have been able to retain their szlachta status, but no record of the residence of Stanisław has yet come to light. His son Onufry can be traced to the village of Niechwiedki, just south of Juraciszki, where the death of his daughter Józefa is recorded in 1828. There is then what can best be described as a family mystery. Onufry's grandson, my great-grandfather Ludwik Franciszek, was the owner of Folwark Han our family estate near the village of Ruda Jaworska, in the Province of Nowogródek, some 84 miles south-west of Oszmiana. Given the number of properties and members of the family living along the line Oszmiana – Holszany – Traby - Juraciszki, the question is why did our branch move so far away from the bosom of the family? A possible answer is found in the next chapter.

Revolutionary

1800 – 1883

From having once been the largest country in western Europe, the Polish-Lithuanian Commonwealth finally disappeared from the map in 1795 when, following the two previous partitions in 1772, and 1793, it was completely swallowed up by the three major powers of Russia, Prussia, and Austria. The history is, as might be expected, complex and well beyond the scope of this book. From a family perspective, the area that would have, in previous years, constituted the Grand Duchy of Lithuania, including the Province of Nowogródek, and the nearby Powiat of Oszmiana came under Russian domination, whilst Galicia the area in south east Poland where my father Ludwik was born, was occupied by the Austro-Hungarian Empire. It was not until after the First World War, that Poland again became an independent sovereign nation in November 1918.

The three Partitions, were bitterly resisted and resented by the Poles resulting in more than fifteen major battles being fought between 1768 and 1794, predominantly against the Russians, but also against their allies the Prussians and Austrians.

Notwithstanding the fact that after 1795 Russia had granted considerable autonomy to the provinces in the former Polish-Lithuania, with Polish remaining an official language, and the szlachta retaining the same rights and privileges as the Russian nobility, the occupation was never fully accepted by the majority of Poles. As might be expected the considerable tension that existed came to the fore at regular intervals during the ensuing 120 years. The result being a series of bloody but unsuccessful uprisings, in particular those of 1830, 1846, 1848, and 1863.

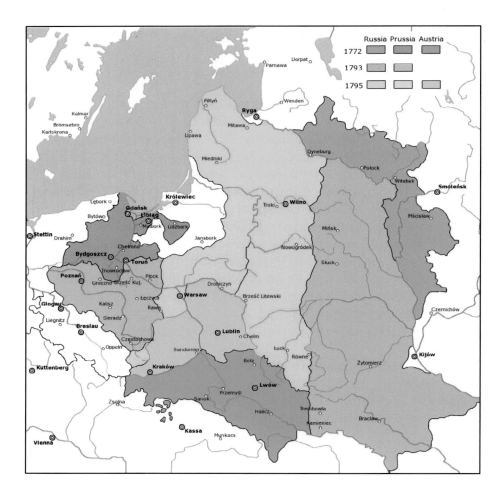

18 Map of the Partitioning of Poland in 1772, 1773, and 1795

The November 1830 uprising began in Warsaw when Polish cadet officers from Poland's military academy revolted. The insurgency was supported in numerous parts of Poland including, what is now Lithuania, Belarus, and western Ukraine.

However, that revolt was not particularly well led or organised and was easily and ruthlessly crushed by the superior Russian forces not least in Polish-Lithuania in general, and the town of

Revolutionary

Onufry 〉 **Franciszek** 〉 Ludwik 〉 Franciszek 〉 Ludwik 〉 Ryszard

Oszmiana in particular. In April 1831, insurgents having occupied the town were pushed back by the Russians, and following a skirmish on the outskirts of the town a detachment of the Finnish Battalion of the Russian Imperial Life-Guards,[55] took punitive action: burning the town and indiscriminately murdering the townsfolk. The one infamous episode, for which the incident is perhaps best remembered occurred when the men, women, and children that had sought refuge in the Dominican Church were massacred by the Russians. The exact number is open to speculation, as is whether it was carried out by the Finnish Battalion or a renegade company of Cossacks. The 'Massacre of Oszmiana' as it became to be known was very quickly romanticised and glorified as a tangible symbol of the sacrifice made by innocent Poles in their resistance against the barbaric Russians.

The massacre was recorded by a number of writers, but salient details differ with each author, not least the actual number of people that died, and even the date on which it took place – given variously as the 3rd April, 10th and 11th April. There is no doubt that the tragic incident did take place, but in a sense the details are of less importance. No opportunity was lost by Polish patriots in publicising the massacre as an important piece of propaganda in the name of the Polish cause.[56] Two particular examples are the poem '*The Slaughter of Oszmiana 1831*' by Konstanty Gaszyński (1809-1866), and a painting depicting the scene in the church by Włodzimierz Łuskina (1849-1894)[57] both reproduced below. It is not insignificant that the poem was written in 1843, and the painting is dated 1891, some twelve, and sixty years respectively after the event.

19 The Massacre in the Dominican Church in Oszmiana -1831 as depicted by Włodzimierz Luskina

Onufry 〉 **Franciszek** 〉 Ludwik 〉 Franciszek 〉 Ludwik 〉 Ryszard

The Slaughter of Oszmiana in 1831
by Konstanty Gaszyński

At the Oszmiana church, on the second Sunday in April, the
Bell called for morning prayers,
And the people gathered in crowds, begged the Lord for pans,
For protection for Poland and Lithuania!

In Christ's sanctuary, you make no difference,
The peasant and the nobleman have entered one door;
With them, wives and mothers, like angels, their children,
and like roses, noble ones!

The priest, bowed, for years, before the altar, the
sacred rite of the church was ending
- And the voice of mocks and lords, with the dissonance of organs,
Flown in the sky on the wings of an angel!

The clang of weapons and arrows in the city sounded, the
cobblestones hummed under the horses' howls - the
door is already screaming - and a wild crowd of Circassians
He ran into the church with a dagger drawn.

And captors without a soul, whose hearts are not moved by
 Su crying child, an old man than a white coat,
not buried in the work of thine - as in the church throughout the
corpses only in the blood were pouring!

Babies dying, forgive the robbers for Lord Sacrilege
over Your temple!
Because these Tsar soldiers, just like the Roman murderers,
They did not know what they were doing!

But in the hour judgment, let your anger not pass away,
Let your lightning punish it,
What let these hordes, what these murders commanded
And smears with innocent everyday blood!

And widows, old people and children, let the martyr's swarm
next to the victims of the first uprising,
What under Russian iron, under Tsarist order,
Lay in Prague and in ruins Humanity!

To soothe the wrath of heaven, if you need more blood,
After all, the periphery flowed -
To wash away perpetual sins, take ours for Christ!
But mother, come back life!

Our people serve you faithfully, curse you,
do not punish him no more, hear the humble cry!
It has already been over half a century,
Poland is suffering - and waiting for Your Mercy, Lord!

Aix, 1843

The exaggeration and appropriation of the events in Oszmiana to promote a political cause should not detract from the impact they had on the Gan family. In the contemporaneous memoir edited by Wrotnowski,[58] although somewhat less partisan, but still very emotive, it states that during the course of Russian troops going from door to door seeking out those that had participated in the insurrection, some eighty people were indiscriminately slaughtered regardless of their involvement, perceived or otherwise. He identifies the names of nine people killed in this way including that of my cousin Tomasz Gan.[59]

The outcome of the failure of the 1830 Uprising had, as might be expected, major repercussions. The Russians imposed severe restrictions on the population of Lithuania, including the closure of the University of Wilno,[60] which had up to that time not only been the largest university in the Russian Empire, but most significantly because Polish was the language used for teaching. Those convicted of involvement in the uprising were, either executed – ten were condemned to death by decapitation, and a further 350 by hanging - imprisoned, or exiled to Siberia, – but most had already left the country; over 3,000 estates were confiscated as a consequence, and some 10,000 officers were given hard labour or reduced to the ranks.[61]

20 Dworek Mickiewiczów in Zaosia by Napoleon Orda c1875

The failure of the Uprising also led to the start of what became known as the *Wielka Emigracja* or Great Emigration with a considerable number of influential Poles, including politicians, intellectuals, writers, musicians and other professionals preferring to live a life in exile, predominantly but not exclusively in France or England. These included such famous luminaries as Prince Adam Czartoryski (1740-1861), Fryderyk Chopin (1810-1849), and Adam Mickiewicz (1798-1855). The fame and standing of the latter may be summed up in describing Shakespeare as England's Mickiewicz. Mickiewicz has a particular significance because his family estate of Zaosie was also in Nowogródek some 37 miles from our family estate at Ruda Jaworska. One of his best-known works is *Pan Tadeusz, or the Last Foray in Lithuania, a Tale of the Nobility 1811-1812, in Twelve Books of Verse.*[62] Deemed by many to be the last great epic poem in European literature, it was first published in Paris in 1834.[63] [64] In one sense, it is a matter of some regret that the book is still compulsory reading in all Polish schools, which has no doubt had the effect of putting off most Poles from reading it for pleasure, in much the same way as the works of Shakespeare in England. One of the best and most recent English translations is by Bill Johnston. It is well worth reading as it paints a very vivid picture of the landscape, life, times, and circumstances of our own family, during this particular difficult period in Polish history.[65]

The restoration of Polish sovereignty remained the underlying reason for the uprising, and the principal objective both in Poland and overseas. It led to the creation of a number of organisations, to help fulfil that dream. In England, The Literary Association of the Friends of Poland (LAFP) was formed in 1832, by Thomas Campbell, a Scottish poet, who was succeeded as President by the British politician, Lord Dudley Coutts Stuart (1803-1854) a passionate advocate of Polish independence and an influential member of Parliament from 1830 until his death in 1854.

21 Lord Dudley Coutts Stuart (1803-1854)

The headquarters of the LAFP was at 10 Duke Street, St. James's London, now the headquarters of Supreme Council of the Ancient and Accepted Rite for England and Wales, a large world-wide Masonic organisation. The Masonic connection is continued as Lord Dudley Coutts Stuart was one of the first

Revolutionary

Onufry 〉 **Franciszek** 〉 Ludwik 〉 Franciszek 〉 Ludwik 〉 Ryszard

members of the Polish National Lodge No. 546, founded in 1846, by Polish Freemasons exiled in England, together with a number of English supporters, who were sympathetic to the cause of Polish independence. The Lodge has always worked in English, and although any discussion of politics in lodges is banned in English Freemasonry, the reason for the establishment of the Lodge was abundantly clear. Its formation was attended by no less than the Earl of Zetland, and the Earl of Yarborough, the Grand Master, and Deputy Grand Master respectively. The Grand Master granted the members the rare

22 Polish National Lodge Members' Jewel

privilege of being able to wear a members' breast jewel, the Polish white eagle, in silver, surmounted with a golden crown and suspended by a ribbon in the colours of the 'Virtuti Militari', the highest Polish military honour awarded for heroism and courage.

As so often happens in Polish politics, factions are readily formed. There is a long-standing Polish joke that if you put two Poles together, within minutes you will have at least three political parties. For some it remained a question of Polish Sovereignty, and the removal of foreign oppression, whilst for others there was in addition a desire for greater social equality, put in very simple terms the predominantly right of centre 'whites' and the socialist 'reds'.

A number of groups representing a range of factions were formed to promote the cause for Polish freedom both at home and abroad. Those overseas included the *Towarzystwo Demokratyczne Polskie or TDP (*Polish Democratic Society), in which serial insurgents such as Ludwik Mierosławski (1814-1878)[66] were actively involved. One underground group in Poland worthy of note was the *Zwiazek Bratni Mlodziezy Litewskiej* (Brotherhood of Lithuanian Youth), formed by two brother, Franciszek, and Aleksander Dalewski. It was based and active in Wilno from 1846 to 1849, and its aims were primarily the encouragement of Polish nationalism, opposition of the Tsarist regime in general, and the prevention of any further Russification.[67]

One person known to have taken a leading role and to be actively involved with the various dissident groups in Wino, including the Brotherhood, was Franciszek Gan.

The Brotherhood drew its support primarily from students, and young intellectuals, but it clearly struck a chord and grew quite rapidly, by widening its appeal to include young working people and artisans. Its influence was further increased as it absorbed other local groups, with fundamentally more radical aims, such as that led by Michal Mikutowicz in Wilno, and further afield that led by Michal Boki in Minsk.

Revolutionary

Onufry 〉 **Franciszek** 〉 Ludwik 〉 Franciszek 〉 Ludwik 〉 Ryszard

Whilst the Brotherhood may well have considered itself a radical organisation, the prospect of an insurrection was never more than a future aspiration. What changed was what became known as the *Springtime of the Peoples* or the *Spring of Nations* in Europe in 1848 when, during the course of that year, some 350 different insurrections and revolutions were recorded world-wide.[68] This led to a change of direction within the Brotherhood and plans were drawn up for an uprising against the Tsarist government to take place the following year in 1849. The objective of the proposed insurrection was straight forward - the establishment of an independent Polish republic, in which all citizens would be equal, and the abolition of serfdom. The insurrection was planned to start in Wilno, and simultaneously in surrounding provinces on Easter Monday in April 1849. The organisers must have been extremely naïve if they thought that an insurrection of that scale could be kept secret. The Russian authorities were well aware of the plans by early March, and mass arrests quickly followed. The defendants, some two hundred in number, mostly aged between eighteen and nineteen, were imprisoned whilst the authorities carried out their investigations, and the trials finally took place between February and April 1850. As might be expected the sentences handed out were most severe, and included:

Franciszek Dalewski [69]   (1825-1904)   aged 24
Sentenced to death – reduced to
15 years hard labour in Siberia
Aleksander Dalewski [70]   (1827-1862)   aged 22
10 years hard labour in Siberia
Florjan Danowski [71]   (1822-1903)   aged 27
8 years hard labour in Siberia
Edward Żeligowski [72]   (1816-1864)   aged 33
8 years exile in Siberia
Bronisław Lutkiewicz   an army officer
reduced to serve in the ranks
One name conspicuously absent from the list above is that of Franciszek Gan. Every family has gaps in its history or

episodes, or even skeletons in cupboards, that merit some form of explanation, and as will be seen the Gan family, is no different in that respect.

Two particular issues that have remained unanswered to date are: why, when so many properties and branches of the Gan family were settled in and around Oszmiana, should suddenly our particular branch become the owners of an estate some 80 miles to the south west in the neighbouring Province of Nowogródek?

The second issue relates to the fact relayed by my great-uncle Josef to my father in 1963 that my great-grandfather Ludwik Franciszek, and his father Franciszek Kazimierz, both signed themselves, as Gieysztor-Gan on documents until the end of the first world-war – but gave no indication as to why.

I believe that the answer to both conundrums may be answered by reference to the series of events described both above and below, and the key to which lies with Jakób Gieysztor (1827-1897)[73] who rose to prominence in the 1863 Uprising as the putative President of the Provisional Government of Lithuania, and whose memoirs were published in 1913,[74] in which he makes the following specific reference to the events of 1849 in Wilno in general, as well as his involvement, and that of Franciszek Gan in particular.

> 'While still at the university, I encountered the Dalewski brothers, Franciszek and Aleksander - they, after finishing at the Wilno Gymnasium [Grammar School], surrounded themselves with young people, encouraging them to work, but this association turned into a conspiracy. One day, in the spring of 1849, I was in Kiejdanach,[75] with Franciszek Gan, a school friend of the Dalewskis', and a tutor of my uncle's sons, where we met Danowski. I saw Danowski once in Wilno at the Dalewskis'. He handed me some papers, proposing that I start an uprising in Kaunas,

and a second set of papers for Bronisław Lutkiewicz with a similar proposition for the Russian district. He told us that everything was ready, that prominent people are taking part in the conspiracy, and the purpose of the insurrection was to cause a diversion so that Russians would not go to Hungary. He cited Mierosławski visiting Wilno[76] and similar initiatives. Seeing that Gan was too much interested, I told him to go back to Zabieliszek[77] (my uncle's estate), and I waited for Danowski to return to the bridge when straight away I returned to him both sets of papers. To his pleading and pressure, I answered firmly: "if and when two come into the field, I will be third, but I do not have enough influence that I can count on that will pull in the masses behind me, and more importantly nor can I see the possibility of anything being accomplished in the country today." We both parted in a state of irritation, he because of my refusal, and I for the calamity that threatened the country.

I hurried to Zabieliszek and immediately sent Gan to Wilno[78] to talk to Franciszek Dalewski, and if necessary with Edward Żeligowski. It was too late. Francis, as is often the case with leaders, was caught up in the maelstrom of events. Arrests and court hearings began. Sacrifices for the country increased, the strength of the character of the two Dalewski brothers shone through. Gallant Danowski did not say anything about either me or Gan, and I survived, although I was still anxious for a whole year because there is no satisfaction in dying for something in which one does not share the same convictions.

In Kiejdanach I Immediately learned that, due to the indiscretion of one of Czapski's officials, there was already loud talk about the uprising in Wilno earmarked for Easter. General Yuri Jewrieinow said exactly the same to Karol Zabielle in Opitołokach. The

Dalewskis and Danowski went to Siberia. The family, newly deprived of a father, lost their only help in grown up sons, who were not afraid of work and who knew how to work. Although the conspiracy was undertaken by principled people, it was too premature and ended an era of sacrifice and secret plots.'

The extract from Jakób Gieysztor's memoire refers to the fact that Franciszek was a tutor to the sons of his uncle Stefan, the owner of the Zabieliszek estate. It would also appear that Franciszek took the advice given by Jakób, and by retreating to the Gieysztor estate appears to have avoided arrest for what seems to be a leading role in the proposed insurrection. It is also significant that neither Franciszek or Jakób were betrayed by the Dalewski brothers.

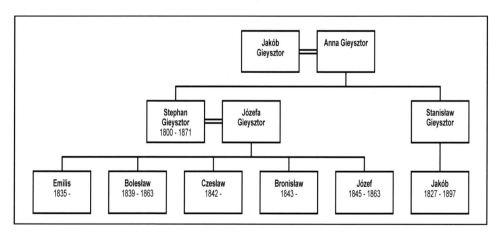

23 Extract from the Gieysztor Family Tree

As can be seen from the extract of the Gieysztor family tree, the likelihood is that Franciszek would at the time have been the tutor to Bolesław and Czesław, then aged eleven and seven respectively, rather than Emilis who, at the age of fourteen, would have been at secondary school. What is significant is that Bolesław and Józef were both killed taking part in the 1863 uprising, in which of course their nephew Jakób was also

Onufry 〉 **Franciszek** 〉 Ludwik 〉 Franciszek 〉 Ludwik 〉 Ryszard

actively involved. The adoption by Franciszek of the double-barrelled name of Gieysztor-Gan, is I believe, directly related to his relationship with the family in general and Bolesław in particular. The exact reasons are of course open to speculation. It may have been guilt on the part of Franciszek – having escaped prosecution following the events of 1849, in which there is little doubt that he was heavily involved – whilst the Gieysztor family suffered the double loss with the death of two sons. It may also be that in living with the family and fulfilling the important role of a tutor a genuine bond had been established between him and the family as a whole. Whatever the underlying reasons might have been there is little doubt that for Franciszek to embrace the Gieysztor name, would have required the approval of that family.

There remains the issue of the Folwark Han estate. It will be recalled that following the 1831 Uprising many Szlachta families lost their estates, and consequently their livelihoods by their involvement, however slight. There is every possibility that the Gan family wishing to avoid a similar occurrence would have deemed it sensible to send Franciszek as far away as possible from the family estates and where better than Ruda Jaworska, a village in the county of Nowogródek 80 miles south west of Oszmiana, and 87 miles south of Wilno. There is also the question of how a tutor in his middle or late twenties would be able to afford a 26-hectare (64 acre) estate, which is likely to have been purchased on his behalf by members of the Gan family or perhaps just as likely the Gieysztor family, which would further explain the Gieysztor-Gan connection.

No record has been found to date as to how and when Folwark Han came into the ownership of the family. It is shown on the map detailing the location of all the various Gan properties, and a more detailed location map, and plan of the estate of 1883 are shown below. It is worth commenting that on this Polish map dated 1930,[79] and on others including one of German origin published in 1914,[80] it is recorded as Folwark Han rather than Gan.

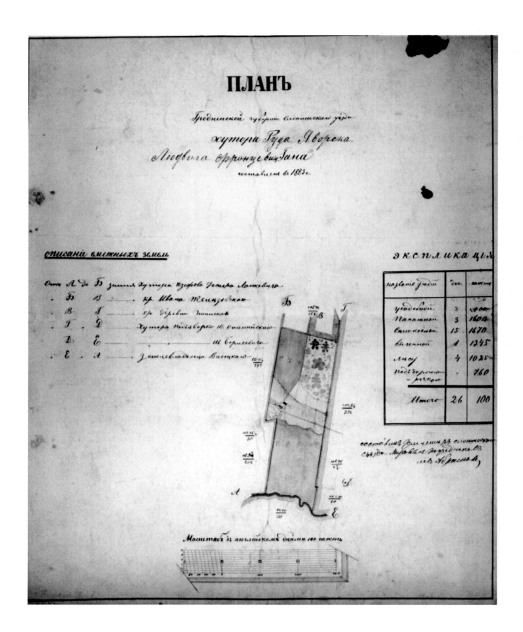

24 Plan of the Folwark Han Estate - 1883

Revolutionary

Onufry 〉 **Franciszek** 〉 Ludwik 〉 Franciszek 〉 Ludwik 〉 Ryszard

Given that Poland only became independent again in 1918, the retention of the name 'Han' is unusual to say the least, and may well have been a symbolic gesture on the part of Franciszek aimed against the Russians. There are two detailed plans of the estate in possession of the family, one in Russian drawn up in 1883 which I believe was part of the probate following the death of Franciszek, and one dated 1929 in Polish, drawn up in similar circumstances following the death of his son Ludwik Franciszek. There is no reference to the name of the estate on the former, only its location near Ruda Jaworska, but on the latter the name is given as Folwark Han, despite the fact that following the end of the Russian occupation in 1918 the family retained the name Gan rather than reverting to the pre-1795 version of Han. Having stated all that I may have misread the situation and there is of course a possibility that Folwark Han was already in the possession of the family prior to the 1795 partition and hence kept the old-style name until 1939. I am equally sure that records in Vilnius would be able to help resolve the matter one way or the other.

The extract from the family tree that follows shows how little detail is currently known about Franciszek's immediate family members. Insofar as Folwark Han is concerned it would appear that Franciszek was the sole owner and that on his death it was inherited by my great-grandfather Ludwik Franciszek, notwithstanding the fact that Franciszek appears to have had at least two brothers and three sisters, and Ludwik Franciszek, two sisters.

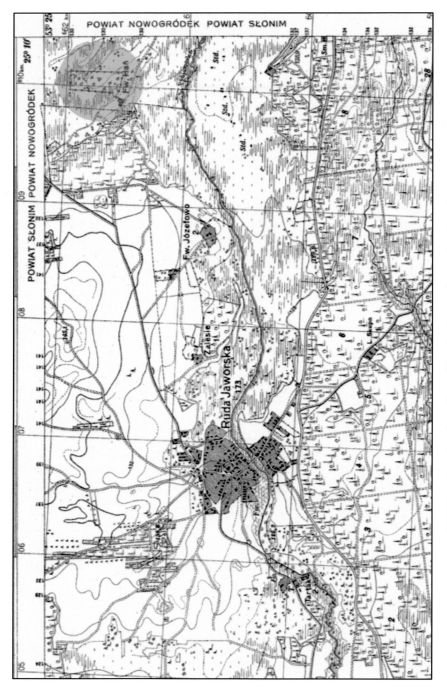

25 Map showing location of Ruda Jaworska and Folwark Han

Revolutionary

Onufry 〉 **Franciszek** 〉 Ludwik 〉 Franciszek 〉 Ludwik 〉 Ryszard

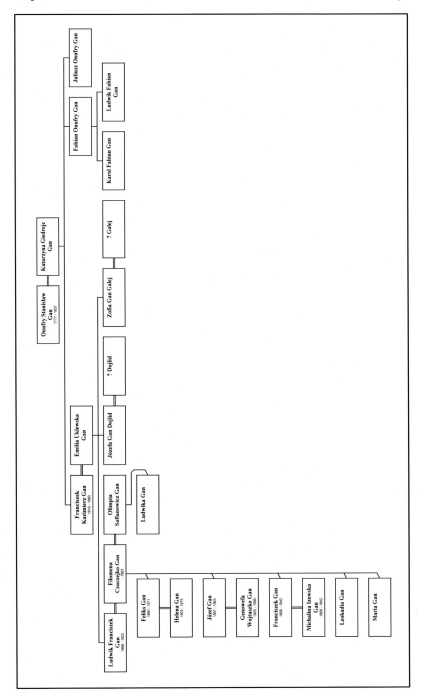

26 Family Tree Excerpt showing the immediate family of Franciszek Kazimierz Gan

My father relates, in a note made in 1963, that when he raised the subject with his own uncle, Józef, the latter was rather vague in his recollection of the names of his great-uncles, i.e. Franciszek's brothers, and the names of the husbands of his own aunts; which could be taken to either reinforce my earlier point about Franciszek's 'exile' from the rest of the family in Oszmiana or a lack of interest on the part of my great-uncle.

In the same note my father states that Ludwik Franciszek who had been hoping to train as a lawyer was somewhat resentful that he had to curtail his studies to return to Folwark Han to take over the running of the estate because his mother was not able to cope following the death of his father. There was also some suggestion that it may have been associated with Franciszek's exile in Siberia – which would have some resonance given his previous history. Given Franciszek's level of involvement in the 1848 Uprising, his friendship with Jakób Gieysztor, who had such a prominent role in the 1863 Uprising, it would be surprising if Franciszek did not play some part himself. Regrettably there is no further information or amplification – yet another family mystery. I estimate that Franciszek died in or about 1883, hence the need of the plan shown above, in all probability for probate purposes. The dates fit because it would make Ludwik Franciszek at least seventeen years old at the time, and therefore a considerable undertaking for him. It will be recalled that during the Russian occupation it was necessary for members of the Szlachta to register their status as such on a regular basis, not least to safeguard their own interests. A copy of such a certificate of confirmation in the name of Ludwik Franciszek and dated 1885 is in the family archive, together with a copy of the passport issued to him in 1898. Travel within Russia at this time was severely restricted and hence the essential passport that would have been a privilege granted to relatively few people.

Farmers

1883 – 1918

As described above Ludwik Franciszek inherited Folwark Han as a working grange-farm[81] in about 1883, which then consisted of 26 hectares (64 acres). Given that his eldest son Feliks was born in 1890 it is not unreasonable to suppose that he would have been married by at least 1889 at the age of twenty-three. Further children followed: two boys Józef in 1894 and my grandfather, Franciszek in 1899, together with two daughters - Leokadia and Maria, although we do not yet know their dates of birth. Little further is known about Ludwik - if his photograph is anything to go by – a formidable character, other than, following the death of his first wife Filomena in 1905 when my grandfather was six, he married Olimpia Safjanowiczów, who appears to have had two daughters from a previous marriage – Maria and Weronika – and with whom he had a further daughter Ludwika. If there is a such a thing as a clichéd story regarding wicked step-mothers, then this is yet another to add to the list, and which came to a head following

27 Ludwik Franciszek Gan c.1920

the death of my great-grandfather at the relatively young age of fifty-eight in 1923.

In 1922 Ludwik made his last will and testament, a copy of which is in the family archive. It is couched in terms that makes it clear that relations between Olimpia and the three sons were strained to say the least, and one that continued to fester for sixteen years following the death of Ludwik in 1923. In 1927, there was a legal dispute between the brothers and their step-sister Ludwika. It was not until 1929, that the ownership of Folwark Han was confirmed and divided equally between the three brothers, and matters were only completely resolved following the death of Olimpia in 1939.

The main points contained in the will dated 20 October 1922, and formally certified in June 1925, is that Ludwik's second wife Olimpia was to retain the same rights to the assets of the Estate as during his lifetime, but in the event of any dispute with the three sons she was to be given control of 5 morgi[82] of meadow, and 1 morg of ploughed land, bordered by the river in the south, the land in the east belonging to Borysiewioz, the land in the west belonging to Józefa Okołowa, and the rest of the Estate to the north, which after her death would revert to the three sons. In addition, Olimpia received two cows (one jet black, one mottled red); two one-year old bulls; a ten-year old bay mare with harness, together with the use of the farmhouse and buildings. The three daughters Maria, Weronika, and Ludwika were granted, at the time of their choosing (presumably as a dowry), two cows, two sheep, and half-a-million Polish Marks.[83] The rest of the livestock, cows and horses together with all the farm equipment was left to the three sons.

It would appear that Maria and Weronika, had previously received their original bequest, because in March 1927, four years after the death of Ludwik an agreement was reached between the three brothers and their half-sister Ludwika Konstantynowiczowa, née Gan, in respect of her original bequest. Whereby in lieu of the 'two cows, two sheep, and 500,000 Polish marks', she would receive a sum of 1,200 Złoty to be paid in three instalments - 600 Zł. on 19 March 1927, 400 Zł. on 1 August 1927, and 200 Zł. on 1 January 1928. It rather sounds like Ludwika on the basis that she was one of the four children of Ludwik, may have been making some form of claim on the estate. That seems to be borne out by the fact that the terms agreed between her and the three brothers certainly seem very generous, when compared with that originally contained in the Will of 1922. Matters seem to have reached a satisfactory conclusion because there is a copy of a receipt dated 6 July 1928 signed by Ludwika Konstantynowiczowa, in respect of 1,200 Zł. together with confirmation that she relinquishes any claim she might have against Feliks and Józef [84] arising from the Will.

Later that month, on 25 July, presumably as part of the probate procedure, an Arbitration Tribunal decision was made regarding the ownership of the Estate, and in the September a copy of the decision submitted to the Tax Office for collection of the appropriate fees of 935 Zł., and for an enforceable title to be issued subject to the submission of a Land Office permit.

It is not until June 1929 that the Town Court in Zdzięcioł finally granted the title of the Estate to Feliks, Józef, and Franciszek. Following which on 20 June a meeting was held on the Estate in the presence of the mayor of Zdzięcioł, when the formal arbitration document, was read out-loud, and subsequently signed two days later, confirming the division of Folwark Han between the three brothers, Feliks, Józef, and Franciszek, with each receiving 7.77 hectares (19 acres).

The estate was divided into a series of strips, reminiscent of the English medieval open-field system. The details of the allocation, are shown on map of the estate dated 1928, with Franciszek receiving the plots of land labelled No.: 3, 2a, 3b, and 3c.

Gan – is that a Polish name?

28 Plan of the Folwark Han Estate 1928

66

Farmers

Onufry 〉 Franciszek 〉 **Ludwik 〉 Franciszek 〉** Ludwik 〉 Ryszard

It is not clear, after all these years, whether there was any tension between the brothers over the division of the estate, or whether it was simply a way of arriving at a fair division of land that varied considerably in composition and quality. The public nature of the announcement of the division may well have been with a view to of avoiding the difficulties encountered with both Olimpia and Ludwika. The total area of the estate amounted to a little over 23 hectares (59 acres), with Franciszek being an 'absent landlord' living in Buczacz, it seems to have fallen to Feliks to have general oversight of the estate.

The official plan shows an area of 28.2 hectares, so there appears to be a discrepancy of just over 5 hectares (13 acres). One reasonable presumption is that part of the balance was still being held by Olimpia as specified in the original Will, - 5 morgi of meadow, and 1 morg of ploughed land – amounting to some 4 hectares, that leaves approximately one hectare (2½ acres) still to be accounted for. A family anecdote recounted on more than one occasion by my father was that during his annual visits to Folwark Han, when discussions took place about the shortage of money my step-great-grandmother would quip that the solution was simple – 'just sell another field' – which may well account for the discrepancy in acreage described above.

No sooner had the three brothers been formally registered as the rightful owners of the Estate than a meeting was called on 26 July 1928 of all the inhabitants of the local commune that formed the villages and hamlets, surrounding the estate, known as the Rzepiszcze Cluster – as shown in the map below. It was chaired by none other than the mayor, Antoni Maciuk. At the meeting it was unanimously agreed, by the nineteen[85] of the twenty-nine inhabitants present, who had the right to vote, that Antoni Maciuk and Feliks Gan should, as their representatives, seek permission to register the land of the commune including the pastures, forests and thickets to enable hunting to take place under the auspices of the Hunting Association in Zdzięcioł, for the period 1928 to 1933. The total area involved was some 621.45 tithes[86] (671 hectares - 1,658 acres) which gives some indication of the size of the initiative and its importance to the local community. It also demonstrates that the Gan family was trusted to be playing an active part in local affairs.

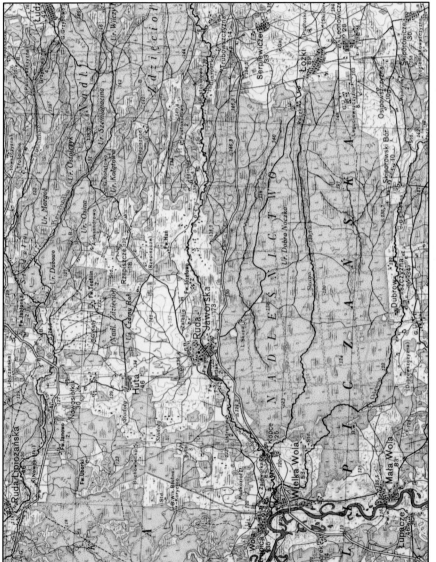

29 Map showing the location of Folwark Han and the Rzepiszcze Cluster

Onufry 〉 Franciszek 〉 **Ludwik 〉 Franciszek 〉** Ludwik 〉 Ryszard

Family documents demonstrate that matters relating to the Estate continue to be dealt with at a formal level, perhaps an indication that there may have been insufficient trust between the three brothers and/or their step-mother, or simply to avoid any possibility of future recriminations as exhibited previously with Ludwika. In August 1931 a Certificate was issued by the Town Court in Zdzięcioł, at the request of Feliks and Franciszek (but not seemingly Józef), indicating that, following the death of Ludwik Gan, Folwark Gan consisted of about 22 tithes (23.76 hectares – 59 acres) of various types of land, with a total value of about 11,000 Zł.[87] There does not appear to be any obvious reason for the need of the certificate, other than perhaps tax related, or establishing an agreed base-line for future transactions between the brothers.

It will be recalled that Franciszek had been living away from the Estate for a number of years so it is of little surprise when in September 1932 Franciszek formally agreed to lease to Feliks plot 3c, amounting to 1.4053 hectares to enable him to grow rye for a period of two years from September 1932 to September 1934. The rent was agreed as the equivalent of 12 pudy[88], in either roasted or natural grain, and amounts to about £100[89] in today's money.

Although there is no direct evidence, it would appear that Olimpia died in 1939, because the land that she retained under the terms of the Will of Ludwik, some four hectares came back into the ownership of the three brothers. In July of that year Józef agreed to buy Franciszek's one third share of the reverted land, 1.34 hectares (3 acres). The sum fixed was 800 Zł. in gold to be paid by 1 July 1941, and in the case of the sale not proceeding for reasons beyond the control of either party Franciszek would return the 800 Zł. to Józef. Needless to say, the terms of the transaction were detailed in a document sworn in front of a Notary Public in Zdzięcioł, and as far as is known Franciszek never received the money. As the British Prime Minister, Harold Macmillan, is reputed to have said 'events, dear boy, events'.

Following the outbreak of the second world war in September 1939, great-uncle Józef was initially imprisoned in Brest, He was sentenced[90] by the Soviets on 10 February 1941, and on 11 June 1941 commenced hard labour at the Vorkuta Gulag in northern Siberia, which lies beyond the Arctic Circle; where winter lasts eight months and the average July temperature is around 14 degrees. He remained at the Gulag until 25 February 1942 when, under the terms of the agreement reached between Stalin and the western powers, he was able to join the Polish Army under General Anders, initially transferred to Buzuluk, and ultimately to Palestine. After the war he decided not to return to Poland despite entreaties from his wife, who had remained in Poland, and lived in exile in Bradford, England keeping in close contact with his nephew, my father, until his death in 1963.

Insofar as my other great-uncle Feliks is concerned there is very sparse information about him both prior to and subsequent to the end of the War. My understanding is that he eventually left the Estate, presumably after 1934, to pursue other professional interests that may have included journalism. There is a document file in the family archive that states that in 1954 he was registered as being 70% incapacitated for work. He remained in Poland, where he died in 1971.

There is no evidence remaining of Folwark Han at Ruda Jaworska on contemporary satellite images on 'Google Maps', the property would have been confiscated by the Soviet authorities when that part of Poland was incorporated into Belarus in 1945.

Olimpia Saffanowicz Gan

Ludwika Gan

Maria Gan

Leokadia Gan

Michalina Izewska Gan 1899 - 1942

Filomena Czuczełko Gan - 1905

Franciszek Gan 1899 - 1940

Ludwik Franciszek Gan 1866 - 1923

Genowefa Wojtuszko Gan 1905 - 1996

Józef Gan 1897 - 1963

Helena Gan 1903 - 1975

Feliks Gan 1890 - 1971

Ludwik Gan 1926 - 2011

Czesława Gorzelnik Gan 1928 -

Czesław Feliksa Gan 1929 - 1984

Hermina Fromwald Gan

Roman Gan 1933 - 2003

Teresa Sierzputowska Gan 1944 -

Teresa Gan Tomaszewski 1939 -

Eligiusz Eugeniusz Tomaszewski 1925 - 2007

Stanisława Gan Zabłocki 1929 - 1998

Alfons Zabłocki 1930 - 1992

Irena Gan Leptuch

Jan Leptuch

Eugeniusz Gan

Stanisława Kobylarz Gan

Cezara Gan Kędra

Eugeniusz Kędra

Emil Gan 1937 -

Emilia Gan

Bogdan Gan 1940 -

Regina Gan 1945 - 2011

Zygmunt Gan

30 Family Tree Excerpt showing the descendants of Ludwik Franciszek Gan

Hero

1919 – 1940

Franciszek Ludwik Gan was born on 10 March 1899, the son of Ludwik Franciszek and Filomena, on the family estate, Folwark Han, near Ruda Jaworska, in the north eastern Province of Nowogródek.[91] The youngest of three brothers, Feliks 1890, and Józef 1894, he also had an elder sister Maria, as well as a younger sister Leokadia and, half-sister Ludwika, together with two step-sisters, Weronika and Maria [dates of birth yet to be confirmed].

As yet nothing is known about his early life or education, other than he did not go to University, and appears to have joined the Polish army straight from secondary school.[92]

His mother Filomena, died in 1905 when Franciszek was six. From the terms of his father's Will written in 1922, it is clear, as described above, that there were tensions between the three brothers and their step-mother Olimpia, who brought with her two daughters, from her previous marriage.

Given the friction within the family and especially with his step-mother, together with the prospect that an estate of 28 hectares could not easily support such a sizable family, it is no surprise that Franciszek appears to have decided to join the Polish Army, most probably at the age of eighteen.

This is supported by a number of factors, not least some early photographs of him in uniform, from which it is able to discern that he wore 'collar-snakes' – the rank of which is likely to be that of a Private, aiguillettes and cords off the left shoulder,[93] and two different regimental badges. Although both the angle and quality of the photographs are not ideal it just possible to identify the first badge as that belonging to the Pułk Ułanów Kaniowskich, 6 puł (6th Kaniow Ułan [Light Cavalry] Regiment) that was formed in 1917 and disbanded in 1919, and which

73

explains the second badge, that of the 6 Pułk Artylerii Polowej (6th Field Artillery Regiment) to which he appears to have been transferred.[94]

31 Franciszek Gan in Army Uniform - c1919

Hero

Onufry 〉 Franciszek 〉 Ludwik 〉 **Franciszek** 〉 Ludwik 〉 Ryszard

32 Franciszek Gan in the uniform of a Senior Constable - post 1934

From a photograph of Franciszek in police uniform, taken some time after 1934 [95], two medals can be identified, both of which were conferred in 1928:

Medal Pamiątkowy za Wojnę 1918–1921
(Commemorative Medal for the War of 1918 – 1921),
awarded to soldiers who fought for Polish Independence between November 1918 and March 1921, and

Medal Dziesięciolecia Odzyskanej Niepodległości
(Medal of the Decade of Regained Independence),
awarded to personnel who, for a minimum period of five years, between November 1918 and November 1928, gave impeccable service in the police, military and other public services.

There are a number of photographs of Franciszek in Police uniform in which he is seen wearing not only the two medals but also the regimental badge of the 6 Pułk Artylerii Polowej. A more detailed description of the two medals, and the two regimental badges are given in Appendix 1.

The Policja Państwowa (Polish State Police) was established in 1919, following Polish independence in 1918. Candidates had to be Polish citizens, aged from 23 to 45, with an impeccable past, good physical fitness, knowledge of the Polish language, and literacy skills.

Franciszek's wedding photograph of 1925 shows him wearing the uniform of a police constable. Given that he became eligible to join the police when he reached the age of 23 in 1922, it follows that he must have become a policeman sometime between 1922 and 1925.

Having joined the army in or about 1917, Franciszek took no active part in the running of the family estate, which appears to have been managed initially by Feliks, and ultimately by Józef. As a consequence, if he was not to return to Ruda Jaworska, Franciszek would have needed to find suitable paid

Onufry 〉 Franciszek 〉 Ludwik 〉 **Franciszek** 〉 Ludwik 〉 Ryszard

employment. Having successfully served in the army, it would be fairly safe to assume that his move from the army to the police was both a natural and comfortable transition.

At present, we do not have any further details about Franciszek's military history, other than that he fought in the Polish-Soviet War of 1919-1921, hence the award of the Medal Pamiątkowy za Wojnę. However, it is known that his regiment fought in several battles in south-eastern Poland, and that after the war it was garrisoned in Stanisławów when, during the time the barracks were being re-built, soldiers were billeted in surrounding villages.

It is no surprise that his first posting as a police constable was to the town of Buczacz (pop. 10,257),[96] less than sixty miles from Stanisławów.

33 Wedding Photograph Franciszek and Michalina - 13 April 1925

It was there that he met and married Michalina Izewska (1899-1942). She was born in the village of Trybuchowce, on the south-eastern outskirts of Buczacz. Her father, Mikołaj Izewski, was born in Brzezany, a town some forty miles north of Buczacz, where he worked as railway engineer. As the railway network expanded he was transferred to Buczacz, where he met his future wife, Zuzanna, my maternal great-grandmother, whose parents were Jan and Katarzyna Turczanski – hence the present-day connection with that branch of the family – see Appendix 3.[97] Sadly, when Michalina was eight Zuzanna died, and Mikołaj subsequently re-married.

Franciszek and Michalina had four children: three of whom were born during their time in Buczacz: my father, Ludwik (1926-2011), Czesiek (1929-1984), and Roman (1933-2003). Teresa (1939-), the youngest child was born whilst the family were living in Koropiec.

In April 1934 Franciszek was promoted to the rank of Senior Constable, and appointed as the Komendant (commander) of the Police Station in Koropiec (pop. 2,353)[98] some 15 miles south of Buczacz. It was during his time there that on 29 August 1938 he was officially commended for the *'diligent and zealous performance of official duties'*, that led to the detection of perpetrators of the scattering of anti-state leaflets, presumably by Ukrainian nationalists, and rewarded with a one-off payment of 50 złoty (£50 in today's money).[99]

On 22 May 1939, at his own request, but without any contribution towards his moving expenses, he was transferred to the post of Komendant of the Police Station in Cebrów (pop. 700) some 10 miles west of Tarnopol, the provincial capital.[100] Given the difference in population, the reason for the move is not clear, but Cebrów was on the main railway line from Lwów, and as such may have been a more demanding posting. It may also have been as a consequence of the events in Koropiec the previous year. There was certainly considerable tension between the Poles and Ukrainians in the area.

Onufry ⟩ Franciszek ⟩ Ludwik ⟩ **Franciszek** ⟩ Ludwik ⟩ Ryszard

Poland having regained its independence in 1918 at the conclusion of the First World War, it was inevitable that after 123 years of occupation its international borders needed to re-defined and ratified. The victorious Allies proposed the so called 'Curzon Line' as the boundary between Poland and the Soviet Union in the east. Suffice it to say neither Poland nor the Soviet Union found the proposition entirely satisfactory and the outcome was the Polish-Ukrainian War of 1918-1919, followed by the Polish-Soviet War of 1919-1921,[101] during which Polish troops were successful in pushing the Russians out of eastern Galicia.

The Soviets pursuit for peace in October 1920, resulted in the Riga Treaty of March 1921. One outcome of which was the re-definition of the Polish-Soviet border, with Poland retaining the former Province of Galicia, that Austro-Hungary had originally seized from Poland in 1772. Other elements of the treaty included Poland's agreement to recognise the Ukrainian Soviet Socialist Republic; and giving guarantees that it would acknowledge and respect the Ukrainian interests in Galicia. The latter never materialised and, as a consequence, Poland would eventually reap the seeds of wrath that it had sown.

Prior to 1939, Lwów[102] was considered one of Poland's cultural capitals, with a population comprising Polish 50% / 16% Ukrainian;[103] whereas in eastern Galicia as a whole, Ukrainians made up approximately 65%, and Poles only 22% of the population.[104]

Between 1919 and 1939, the former Austro-Hungary province of eastern Galicia, comprised three Polish Voivodeships (Provinces), collectively known as Eastern Little Poland (Małopolska Wschodnia), with an ethnic composition summarised as follows:

Lwów	Polish 58% / 34% Ukrainian
Stanisławów	Polish 22% / 69% Ukrainian
Tarnopol	Polish 49% / 46% Ukrainian.[105]

There had been a long-standing conflict between the Poles and Ukrainians, that was deeply rooted in ethnic, linguistic, cultural, and political differences, not assisted by the fact that the official language throughout Galicia was Polish.

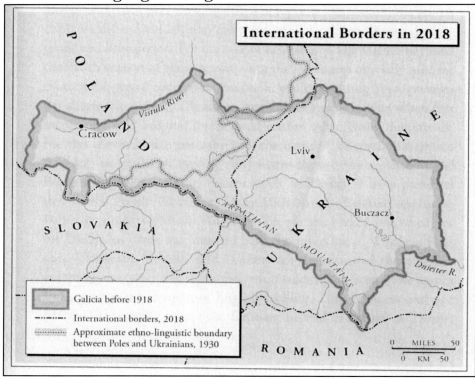

34 Map showing the ethno-linguistic boundary
between Poles and Ukranians - 1930

To attempt to fully explain in any detail the exact nature and intricacies of the conflict is well beyond the scope of this project, but in many respects the map [106] above encapsulates the basic issue, with Poles predominating in the west, with Krakow the ancient capital of Poland as its focus, and the Ukrainians in the east, where Lwów, would have been the natural choice for the principal city of western Ukraine, were it not for the fact that its population was then overwhelmingly Polish.

The present-day border between Poland and the Ukraine follows very closely that of the ethno-linguistic boundary of 1930, and was made possible by the ethnic cleansing started by the Soviets under Stalin in 1939, and completed in 1945.

Franciszek's service with the Polish State Police was based in and around Buczacz in the Province of Tarnopol, whilst my maternal grandparents lived in Kałusz, some forty miles to the west of Buczacz in the Province of Stanisławów; both towns deep in 'Ukrainian' territory.

Whilst Poland had control of its borders it most certainly did not have control of an ever increasingly resentful Ukrainian population, that had growing aspirations to be able to control its own destiny. This manifested itself in the formation of militant groups such as the Organisation of Ukrainian Nationalists (OUN), prepared to use violence to intimidate the innocent members of the Polish population and, with increasing intensity and hostility, carry out acts of terrorism, aimed at the Polish state.

Given the geographical position of Buczacz it is no real surprise that following the outbreak of the Second World War, the Polish population suffered terrible atrocities at the hands of the invading Soviets, ably assisted and supported by their so-called former Ukrainian friends and neighbours.[107] [108]As will be explained their actions had a profound, and catastrophic effect on the lives of my parents, my grandfather, and many other immediate members of the family.

'Katyń' will forever be remembered for the series of mass executions of some 22,000 Poles carried out by the Soviet secret police - the NKVD (People's Commissariat for Internal Affairs - later the KGB) - on the orders of the Soviet Politburo led by Stalin. The executions were carried out in April and May

1940 at a number of different locations including: the prisons at Kalinin [named Tver since 1990], and Kharki. Regardless of the actual location of the various massacres they are now collectively named after the Katyń Forest, where some of the first mass graves were discovered in 1943. [109]

Of those killed, were some 8,000 military officers, 6,000 police officers, and 8,000 members of the Polish intelligentsia. Almost half of the Polish officer corps were murdered including: an admiral, two generals, 24 colonels, 79 lieutenant colonels, 258 majors, 654 captains, 17 naval captains, 85 privates, 3,420 non-commissioned officers, and seven chaplains.[110]

On 1 September 1939, Germany invaded Poland, from the west, and on 17 September 1939, as agreed in the Molotov–Ribbentrop Pact, the Soviet Union invaded Poland from the east. The bulk of the Polish army was concentrated on the western front, and hence with little resistance Tarnopol was occupied on 18 September 1939, and Lwów fell on 22 September 1939.

As a consequence, some 250,000 Polish soldiers were captured by the Soviet Army. Some were released, and some escaped, but 125,400 prisoners were taken into custody by the NKVD,[111] which, having quickly organised a network of reception centres and transit camps, arranged rail transport to a number of prison camps in the western USSR. Military Officers were held at two of the largest camps at Kozelsk (~5000 prisoners) and Starobelsk (~4,000), while Ostashkov (~6750) was used mainly for police officers.[112] In total some 15,570 men were imprisoned in the three camps.[113]

Once at the camps, NKVD officers subjected the prisoners to lengthy interrogations, and attempts to politically indoctrinate them, with the apparent intention of changing their negative attitude towards both communism and the USSR.

Onufry 〉 Franciszek 〉 Ludwik 〉 **Franciszek** 〉 Ludwik 〉 Ryszard

However, it did not bring the expected results, with the majority of prisoners continuing to proudly display their Polish patriotism. At Ostashkov, prisoners were made to face the NKVD Special Conference, a non-judicial body that reached its verdicts by some form of administrative process. It was in fact a selection procedure to determine who would live and who would die. According to NKVD reports, if a prisoner could not be induced to adopt a pro-Soviet attitude, he was declared a "hardened and uncompromising enemy of Soviet authority".[114] By the end of January 1940, the cases of over 6,000 prisoners had been referred to the Special Board. By the end of the following month, the first 600 sentences had been handed down, ranging from 3 to 6 years of hard labour in camps in Kamchatka. The Special Board ceased its work by February 1940, with no further sentences being issued, as its role had been superseded by a new strategy to solve the "problem" of Polish prisoners of war being in the USSR.[115]

There is no doubt that Stalin and the Soviet leadership viewed the Polish prisoners as a "problem", in that they formed the intellectual and military elite of Poland.[116] Their elimination would prevent any significant resistance to Soviet rule, and deprive the Poles of a large pool of potential talent that could, at some point in the future, lead to a revival of the state of Poland.

On 5 March 1940, the Soviet Politburo[117] confirmed the proposal from the People's Commissar for Internal Affairs, Beria, that the prisoners "former officers, officials, landowners, policemen" inside the "special camps" as "avowed enemies of Soviet authority, filled with hatred of the Soviet system" should receive "the maximum sentence – death by firing squad". The decision was signed by those present at the meeting: Stalin, Voroshilov, Molotov, and Mikoyan, and later by two absentees Kalinin, and Kaganovich.[118]

The decision of the Politburo was carried out without any delay. The former Soviet military training camp in Ostashkov was situated on the remote island of Stolbniy on Lake Seliger, twenty miles west of Kalinin, and some six miles from the railway station. From Ostashkov the prisoners were transported by train to the NKVD prison in Kalinin[119] where, beginning on 5 April 1940, they were systematically killed, in a specially prepared cell, by being shot in the back of the head. The bodies were then taken in trucks some 20 miles to Mednoye,[120] and buried in previously prepared trenches. More than 6,300 prisoners previously held at Ostashkov were murdered in this way.[121]

The mass graves in the Katyń and Mednoye forests were discovered by German troops in April 1943. Stalin and the Soviets claimed that Germany was responsible for the massacres. Germany invaded Poland on 1 September 1939, and in accord with the Molotov–Ribbentrop Pact, the Soviet Union invaded Poland on 17 September 1939. It was not until after 22 June 1941, after Germany invaded the Soviet Union, that German troops appeared on Soviet territory, and hence could not have been responsible for the massacre. It was not until 1990 that the Soviets finally officially acknowledged and condemned the killings by the NKVD, as well as the subsequent cover-up by the Soviet government.

My father gave me reason to believe that at the outbreak of the War, my grandfather, Franciszek, lead his team of police officers to safety in Romania - a little over 100 miles from Cebrów - and then returned to his post, where he was shortly after arrested, but I have not yet been able to corroborate that part of the story.

According to the official Russian document, obtained from the Polish Army Archive Office in Warsaw, and now in the family archive, Franciszek Gan was arrested in Cebrów on 28 September 1939, transferred by train to an internment camp in Yukhnov, some 100 miles south west of Moscow, arriving there on 25 November 1939, where he was formally interviewed, and registered on 9 December 1939. The following

Hero
Onufry 〉 Franciszek 〉 Ludwik 〉 **Franciszek** 〉 Ludwik 〉 Ryszard

April, following the decision of the Politburo referred to previously he was transported by train from Ostashkov to the prison at Kalinin where, according to NKVD records he was shot and murdered sometime between the 5th and 7th April 1940,[122] and buried in a mass grave in the forest near Mednoye.

35 NKVD Document No. 012/2 - April 1940

Moscow City - Highly Secret
After receiving this list, you will send without delay to Kalinin for the disposal of the head of the NKVD Board of the Kaliningrad District the following prisoners of war detained in the Ostashkov camp:
[there follows a list of 99 people – including]

82. Witkowiak Władysław s. Wojciecha	— 1090 r.	—,—	—
83. Zajdel Lucjan s. Józefa	— 1907 r.	—,—	2059
84. Gan Franciszek s. Ludwika	— 1899 r.	—,—	3387
85. Szczepanek Alojzy s. Antoniego	— 1903 r.	—,—	5947
	1013 c	— —	5027

Miednoje is now a designated Polish War Cemetery, where the name of Franciszek Gan is recorded in the Cemetery's Official Memorial Book, published in 2005,[123] commemorated together with some 6,300 Poles murdered in similar circumstance.

On 10 November 2007, at the "Katyń We Remember" ceremony of remembrance held in Warsaw, the President of Poland, Jarosław Kaczyński, announced that the sacrifice made by the victims of Katyń massacres was to be formally acknowledged by the State. Accordingly, as a hero of the Polish Nation, Franciszek Gan was posthumously promoted from the rank of Senior Constable to that of a commissioned officer – an Aspirant in the Polish State Police.[124]

There is little more than needs to be added or said about the heroism of Franciszek Gan. His legacy lives on, and is detailed below in the extracts from the Family Tree showing his and Michalina's descendants.

85

36 Map showing the journey made by Franciszek Gan following his arrest in Cebrów and final resting place at Miednoje

Hero

Onufry ⟩ Franciszek ⟩ Ludwik ⟩ **Franciszek** ⟩ Ludwik ⟩ Ryszard

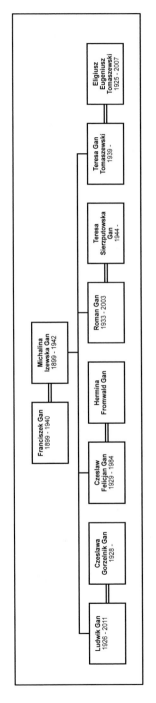

37 Extracts from the Family Tree showing the descendants of Franciszek and Michalina Gan

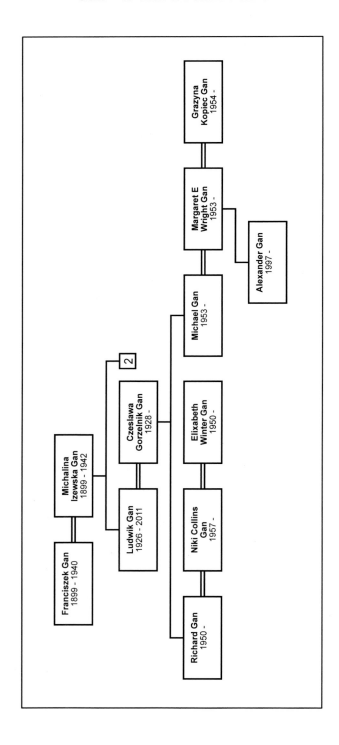

Franciszek Gan
1899 - 1940

Michalina
Izewska Gan
1899 - 1942

Ludwik Gan
1926 - 2011

Czeslawa
Gorzelnik Gan
1928 -

2

Niki Collins
Gan
1957 -

Elixabeth
Winter Gan
1950 -

Michael Gan
1953 -

Margaret E
Wright Gan
1953 -

Grazyna
Kopiec Gan
1954 -

Richard Gan
1950 -

Alexander Gan
1997 -

37a Extracts from the Family Tree showing the descendants of Franciszek and Michalina Gan – Ludwik

Hero

Onufry 〉 Franciszek 〉 Ludwik 〉 **Franciszek 〉** Ludwik 〉 Ryszard

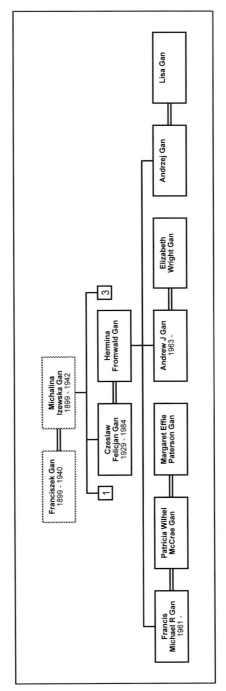

37b Extracts from the Family Tree showing the descendants of Franciszek and Michalina Gan – Czesław

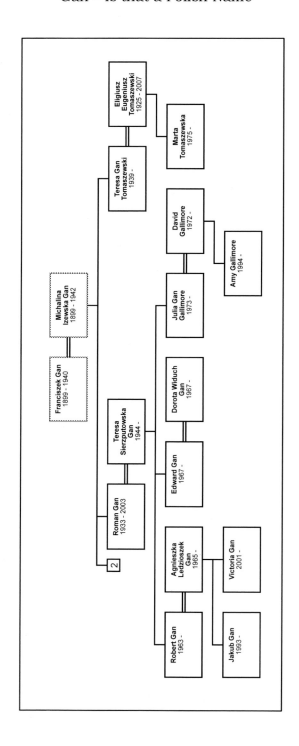

37c Extracts from the Family Tree showing the descendants of Franciszek and Michalina Gan Roman, and Teresa

Political Exile

1940 – 1949

The fate of the families of the Polish prisoners murdered as a consequence of the decision of the Politburo of 5 March 1940, was in fact made three days previously when, on 2 March 1940 the Politburo resolved that:

> *All the families of the former officers of the Polish army, policemen, prison wardens, gendarmes, intelligence agents, former landowners, factory owners and officials of the Polish state apparatus, currently in prison camps, a total of 22,000-25,000 families, are to be deported to the regions of the Kazakh SSR by 15 April, for a period of 10 years.*[125]

As a consequence, over 60,000 people were deported to Kazakhstan, including my father Ludwik (aged 13), his mother Michalina (40), and his siblings, Czesław (Czesiek) (10), Roman (6), and Teresa (1).

The family had moved to Cebrów when Franciszek took up his post as Komendant of the town's Police Station in May 1939. Despite the move, Ludwik continued to attend school in Buczacz, some fifty miles from Cebrów, and the assumption has to be that he boarded there with members of his mother's family, who still lived in the town. In the September of the previous year he transferred from Adam Mickiewicz Junior School, on a scholarship, to the town's famous Gimnazjum (Junior High School).

Soviet soldiers swooped on the family home in Cebrów on Saturday, 13 April 1940. A contemporaneous account from an interview with Czesiek, given whilst in Iran, is contained in the book *Suffer Little Children*, by Irena Wasilewska, published in London in 1946.[126]

"It was a Saturday when they came to us", relates thirteen-year-old Czes[127] (sic) "Mother took little Teresa straight from her bath, wrapped her in an eiderdown and carried her out to the sleigh. We had ten miles to go before we got to the station."

The winter of that year was exceptionally hard. There were frosts of up to 50 degrees below freezing point.

The eventual destination of their enforced deportation was Mayskoye, in north-east Kazakhstan, on the Siberian border, as shown on the map on page 117. One cannot begin to describe the abject misery and deprivation that they encountered and which is perhaps best summed up in the photograph of Ludwik with his siblings, and that of my grandmother, Michalina, one taken in Poland before her captivity and one taken shortly before her untimely death in 1942, where the desperation and sense of desolation is clearly visible in her eyes.

38 Czesiek, Teresa, Ludwik, and Roman in Kazakhstan

39 Michalina in 1939

40 Michalina shortly before her death in 1942

A fundamental change in their circumstances arose in June 1941, following the German invasion of Soviet Russia. As a direct consequence, the Soviets suddenly became so-called Allies.

An agreement was reached with the Soviets in July 1941, and confirmed by the Presidium of the Supreme Soviet on 12 August 1941, for a one-off amnesty enabling those deprived of their freedom, following the Soviet invasion of Poland in September 1939, to be able to join the Polish armed forces.[128]

However, it was not until almost a year later in July 1942, following a forceful and timely intervention by the British government, that long-drawn-out negotiations between the Polish Government in Exile and the recalcitrant Soviets, finally resulted in the agreement from Stalin and the Soviets to allow safe passage of former Polish soldiers and potential recruits to travel to Iran to join up with the British Allied forces.

It should be noted that the original agreement made no provision for the release of any civilians. This came about solely through the intervention of General Władysław Anders who insisted on the evacuation of civilians from the Soviet Union against direct orders from the Polish Government in Exile. In his memoirs he quotes a dispatch from London, signed by the chief of staff General Klimecki:

> *'British authorities are alarmed by the news that families are included in the military transports, that not being within the framework of the evacuation. In view of the great food difficulties in Iran it is necessary to stop absolutely transport of families until agreement is reached with British authorities as it may hamper or restrict military evacuation.'* [129]

Fortunately Anders, who feared that another opportunity for evacuation may never arise, ignored the despatch. His disobedience saved the lives of some 36,000 civilians, including my father and his siblings. As a consequence of his disobedience, there followed an exodus of over 112,000 men, women, and children under his command. It is estimated that over 4,000 soldiers, and innumerable civilians perished whilst awaiting permission from the Soviet authorities for permission to leave Russia. They included my paternal grandmother Michalina who died of typhus in Mayskoye on 11 May 1942,[130] just before the family's departure for Pavlodar, a distance of some 112 miles, the following month. A poignant story surrounding my grandmother's death is that Ludwik realising how ill his mother was, went in search of medication with only a loaf of bread with which to barter. Having managed to get the necessary medicine he returned, only to find that his mother had died in the meantime. He and his brothers used the wood from their bunks to make a crude coffin in which to bury their mother.

Onufry ⟩ Franciszek ⟩ Ludwik ⟩ Franciszek ⟩ **Ludwik** ⟩ Ryszard

The family remained in Pavlodar until September 1942, when they were moved again. This time, the relatively short distance of fifty-six miles to Sherbakty, still in Kazakhstan, but where there was some help from various Polish welfare organisations, including the Red Cross. The next part of the epic journey was a 2000-mile nine-day train journey that started on 22 December 1942, across the length of Kazakhstan, through the whole of Uzbekistan, and Turkmenistan, arriving in Ashkhabad on the border with Iran on New Year's Eve.

The departure of the family from Soviet controlled Kazakhstan, very nearly did not happen, and would not have done so but for Ludwik's tenacity as described by Irena Wasilewska, using the words of Czesiek:

> At last we arrived at Ashkhabad, which lies on the Soviet-Persian[131] frontier. The three-year-old Tereska had come from Kazakhstan with her brothers. These boys, the eldest of whom was Ludwik, aged sixteen, took the most touching care of her. In the midst of their own occupations and amusements, they would run every few minutes to see Tereska, to play with her for a while, or to see if she had eaten her dinner or whether she was crying or if her dress was clean. These children had had great difficulties in getting to Ashkhabad, as I learnt one evening from the fourteen-year-old Czes (sic).
>
> "After Mummy died, they took us to the Polish orphanage at Pavlodar. After a while, the Soviet authorities closed the orphanage, and then our Welfare distributed the orphans among the Polish families in the district. When at last permission came through for Polish orphans to go to India, the four of us were put on the list.

On the appointed day, we went to the railway station. We were just getting into the train, Ludwik was carrying our bundle of things, I had Tereska in my arms and Romek was trotting beside us - when suddenly the lady in charge of us stopped us. She said that the NKVD had crossed our names off the list at the last moment because our name sounded German.[132]

The train started, and we were left behind. We were in absolute despair. There were three other, children left behind on the platform besides us - the NKVD would not let them go because they were Jewish.

Ludwik nevertheless made up his mind that we must get away. He spent several days going round the government offices, begging and entreating them to let us go - and in the end he succeeded in getting permission for us to travel to Ashkhabad. We came here with the next group of children." [133]

What only became known afterwards was that the train on which the family travelled was the very last one allowed to leave Kazakhstan. The family remained in a Polish re-settlement camp Ashkhabad from January 1943 until the June, when they made the next stage of the journey to Tehran in Iran.

On 4 September 1943, in Tehran, Ludwik enlisted in the Polish army or more specifically, the Drugi Korpus Wojska Polskiego (Polish II Corps), 2 Warszawska Brygada Pancerna (2nd Warsaw Armoured Brigade), Pułk 6 Pancerny 'Dzieci Lwówa' (6th Armoured Regiment 'Children of Lwów').

At the same time Czesiek, Roman and Teresa were taken into the care of the Polish Red Cross, eventually being relocated to

Onufry 〉 Franciszek 〉 Ludwik 〉 Franciszek 〉 **Ludwik** 〉 Ryszard

Beirut in Lebanon where Czesiek was enrolled in the sekcja mechaniczna of Junacka Szkoła Kadetów (Mechanics Section of the Young Soldiers Cadet School).

My mother, Czesia (aged 10) and her family shared a very similar experience, to that of my father and his family. She together with her brother Józef (aged 13) and parents Władysław (39) and Julianna (35) were arrested on Wednesday, 14 February 1940 at their home in Kałusz, in eastern Galicia only sixty-five miles from my father's home-town of Buczacz. Their 'crime' apart from being Polish is that the family owned a small-holding and as such were classified as landowners. The family was deported to Łalski, Archangielska in northern Siberia, a journey lasting eleven days in over-loaded cattle trucks, where on arrival they were housed in overcrowded wooden barracks, and were put to work in the surrounding forest. During a twenty-month stay in the camp, over 600 people died out of the 1,700 or so that had originally arrived.

As with the case of my father, my mother's family was eventually given permission to leave Siberia in 1942. Travelling again by cattle truck the journey of over 2,500 miles to the south-eastern borders of Russia as shown in the map on page 118 took several months. The trains were not given any priority, and as such the journey was constantly held up by troop trains carrying reinforcements going west, as well as trains going east carrying wounded soldiers. As might be imagined food was very scarce, and already weakened from their previous travails many died of hunger and disease on the journey, including my maternal grandmother and grandfather who both died of typhus, Julianna in Samarkand, and Władysław, soon after in Guzar. My mother was also hospitalised with the same disease but who, no doubt with age on her side, managed to survive. However, whilst in hospital, she became separated from her brother, my maternal uncle, Józef, and when she had sufficiently recovered made the rest of the journey, orphaned and unaccompanied, under the auspices of the Polish Red Cross.

Having arrived at the port of Krasnovodsk on the eastern shore of the Caspian Sea, she was taken to Pahlavi on the Iranian south shore of the Caspian on the tanker *Molotow*, a journey of over 260 miles in what can best be described as very basic conditions. My mother recalls that during the sailing, two girls in her section of the ship died during the night, their bodies unceremoniously dumped overboard. Once in Pahlavi, the new arrivals were accommodated in tents and huts on the beach. It was whilst playing on the beach that by sheer chance she was reunited with her brother, in what unsurprisingly was a very emotional occasion.

The Polish Air Force mission was formed to select and recruit candidates in Iran for training by the RAF at the No 1 School of Technical Training Halton, near Wendover in Buckinghamshire. Józef was one of 264 boys selected to join the RAF, and to be trained at Halton. From the transit camp at Al Hamra on the Suez Canal, he travelled first to Fayid, and then on to Suez where he boarded the troopship *Stratsmore*, that sailed through the Mediterranean to Liverpool, and then onto Halton, arriving in December 1943.[134]

Meanwhile, Czesia, now aged fourteen travelled via Pahlevi, Tehran, Isfahan, to Ahvaz, then by train to the port of Khorramshahr on the Shatt al-Arab, and from there by ship to Karachi, a journey of over 2,500 miles. Japanese submarines were active in the Indian Ocean, and so ships had to travel as part of a convoy of between six and ten ships protected by corvettes.

The final destination was Valivade in Maharashtra, about six miles from Kolhapur, where a camp had been established to house more than 4,500 Polish refugees, the majority of whom were children. It had two sections: an orphanage for children and teenagers, and a 'civilian area' where women with children could live independently.

Established on the banks of the Panchganga river, the location had been selected partly because of its climate, which was thought to be favourable to Europeans, and perhaps more important it had access to drinking water. The cost of the construction and running expenses, were borne by the Polish Government in Exile. The first group of Poles arrived in Valivade in June 1943 and within a very short period of time it took on the appearance of a small Polish town with an administrative organisation, seven schools for the various age ranges, a post office, church, workshops, hospital, shops, libraries, community centres, and even a fire brigade.[135]

Mother recalls with genuine nostalgia her time at school in India. Having completed her secondary education at the Junior High School, she embarked on two-year Primary School Teachers' training. However, having successfully completed the first year of the course, when the opportunity arose of seeking a new life in England she took it. Arriving in Liverpool on 29 November 1947 from Bombay on the TSS Empire Brent, listed in the ship's manifest as Passenger No. 365 - a student aged 19.

In August 1942 the Polish army had moved from Iran to Iraq, and by August 1943, what had become the Polish II Corps, relocated to Palestine for final training, before being deployed to Italy. Ludwik joined his regiment in Jerusalem, was trained as a radio-operator in Egypt, and landed with the Armoured Brigade in Italy at Taranto in April 1944.

In February 1944 the Polish II Corps under the command of Lieutenant General Anders, become part of the British Eighth Army at Vasto, under General Oliver Leese, with a compliment of some 110,000, and the only force facing the Germans in Western Europe.

In order for Allied forces to capture Rome the only viable route available was to follow the line of Highway 6, that ran through the Liri valley, but which was dominated at its southern entrance by the heights of Monte Cassino, and heavily fortified with German troops.

When Leese offered the opportunity to Anders of the mission to take Monte Cassino, he jumped at the chance. Ander's reasons for doing so were remarkably straight forward, and recorded in his autobiography:

> *"The battle would have international scrutiny and impact; it would be the first face to face battle with the Germans since 1939; capture of Monte Cassino would disprove the Soviet propaganda that the Polish Army was unwilling to fight the Wehrmacht; casualties would probably be the same in a supportive role; it would have great significance for the future of the Home Army of Poland."*[136]

Between January and May, Monte Cassino and the German defences were attacked on at least four occasions by Allied troops. It was not until 16 May, that soldiers of the II Corps launched its final assault and on 18 May, the Polish flag was raised over the ruins of the Benedictine abbey. The objective had been achieved but at an extremely high cost in terms of casualties on both sides.

The Krzyż Pamiątkowy Monte Cassino (Monte Cassino Commemorative Cross) was awarded to Ludwik Gan, and all soldiers of the

41 Krzyż Pamiątkowy Monte Cassino

Onufry 〉 Franciszek 〉 Ludwik 〉 Franciszek 〉 **Ludwik** 〉 Ryszard

Polish II Corps who fought in the battle of Monte Cassino by the Polish Government in Exile.[137]
After Monte Cassino, the II Corps took part in the Battle of Ancona in June/July1944, and finally in April 1945 they were involved in the liberation of Bologna, which ended 14 months of Polish operations during the Italian campaign.

After the Allied victory in Europe in May 1945 the Polish II Corps remained in Italy to provide security arrangements for the Allied Military Government. The Corps had a base in the Apulia Region in 'the heel of Italy' at Casarano, near Lecce. In order to enable young troops to catch up with the education they had inevitably missed, a number of junior high schools were established by the Polish army, including the Drugi Korpus Gimnazjum Ogólnokształcące (2nd Corp General Junior High School) based at Matino. Ludwik attended the school between November 1945 and May 1946, where he undertook the first year of a Pre-Officer Cadet Training Unit (OCTU) course designed to train potential officers in military and other basic skills.

Whilst the soldiers of the Polish Army had been fighting to regain the freedom of their homeland, they had become the victims of an act of gross betrayal on the part of the three major powers in the form of the United States, the United Kingdom, and the Soviet Union. The post-war map of Europe was re-drawn following negotiations between the powers during the course of three conferences held in Tehran, Yalta, and Potsdam respectively in November 1943, February 1945, and July 1945.

It is usually the case that at such conferences the detailed negotiations are mostly carried out by civil servants and officials rather than politicians, but certainly in the case of Potsdam, as is revealed in the original documents and contemporaneous briefing notes, held in the U.S. State Department,[138] the leaders of the three major powers took a very pro-active role.

The significance is heightened because at the final and crucial Potsdam conference President Harry Truman replaced President Franklin Roosevelt, who had died in the April, and Clement Attlee replaced Winston Churchill as Prime Minister, during the course of the conference, the former having won a surprising General Election with a landslide majority of 145 seats, earlier that month. Perhaps more significant was that in the intervening five months between Yalta and Potsdam the Soviet Union managed to occupy Central and Eastern Europe, with the Red Army effectively controlling the Baltic states, Poland, Czechoslovakia, Hungary, Bulgaria, and Romania, as shown in the map on page 102.[139]

Crucially, a communist 'puppet' Polish Provisional Government had been established, in Lublin[140], by the Soviets under Stalin, in a direct challenge to, the Polish Government in Exile, based in London that had been acting since 1939 as Poland's effective sovereign body working under the Polish Constitution of 1935, and with the active support and recognition of the Allied Powers.

It is clear that Stalin and the Soviet leadership had long-term plans for the future control and domination of Poland and eastern Europe. This was amply demonstrated by their decision, in 1940, to deport and execute some 22,000 of Poland's military and intellectual elite in an attempt to deprive Poland of its talent and leadership and by doing so limit any future potential resistance to Soviet rule.

The part of the former Polish–Lithuanian Commonwealth east of the Curzon Line of 1919, known as Kresy or Kresy Wschodnie (Borderlands or Eastern Borderlands) was ceded to Poland as part of the Riga Treaty of 1921 after World War I, and made up approximately half of the territory of pre-war Poland.

Between 1921 and 1939, Kresy consisted administratively, of eight voivodeships including: Nowogródek [The Family Estate -

Onufry 〉 Franciszek 〉 Ludwik 〉 Franciszek 〉 **Ludwik** 〉 Ryszard

Folwark Han at Ruda Jaworska,], Stanisławów [my mother's family home at Kulasz], and Tarnopol [my father's family home at Cebrów, and Buczacz].

Kresy was forcibly annexed by the Soviet Union in September 1939, under the terms of the Molotov–Ribbentrop Pact, see map on page 103.[141]

As part of their ethnic cleansing programme the Soviets deported more than 1,200,000 Poles from Kresy, in four waves of mass deportations. In February 1940: more than 220,000 sent mostly to Siberia, including my mother and her family to Łalski, Archangielska; April 1940, 320,000 sent primarily to Kazakhstan including my father and his family, to Mayskoye; the third wave in June and July 1940 comprised more than 240,000; and the fourth and final wave occurred in June 1941, when some 300,000 were deported. Those deported remained in Russia until 1945 apart from some 100,000 soldiers, and approximately 26,000 civilians allowed to leave in 1941 as part of the 'Ander's Army' to which reference has previously been made.

At the Potsdam Conference, the prospect of the Soviets relinquishing the lands of Kresy forcibly annexed in 1939 was never an issue. As far as Poland was concerned the Soviets were primarily concerned with the liquidation of the London Government in Exile, and the establishment of the Polish Western frontier.[142]

The Soviets adopted a simplistic approach, Poland's loss of territory in the east should be compensated with a similar amount elsewhere, ideally as a form of reparation from defeated Germany. In essence the rationale put forward at Potsdam by the Soviets, and their puppets the Lublin Poles, was that Poland's population was estimated to be about 26 million. In 1931 the average population density had been 83 people per sq. km. On that basis Poland should have access to at least 314,000 sq. km. of land. The amount of land lost in the east to the Soviets by the annexation of Kresy was 184,000 sq. km. leaving Poland with a land deficit of some 214,000 sq. km., or 65% of the total required. The establishment of a new western border for Poland by incorporation of the eastern part of Germany up to the Oder–Neisse line, defined by the Oder and Neisse Rivers, would bring 105,000 sq. km. Although this was still less than required, and 74,000 sq. km. less land than Poland had in 1939, it nevertheless represented a loss for Poland of some 20% compared with a German territorial loss of only 18%.[143]

42 Map showing Soviet territorial gains post 1945

Onufry ⟩ Franciszek ⟩ Ludwik ⟩ Franciszek ⟩ **Ludwik** ⟩ Ryszard

It was only with the greatest reluctance that the British finally consented to the Oder-Neisse Line and it is by no means certain that, but for a change in the British Government in the midst of the Conference, that they would have done so.[144]

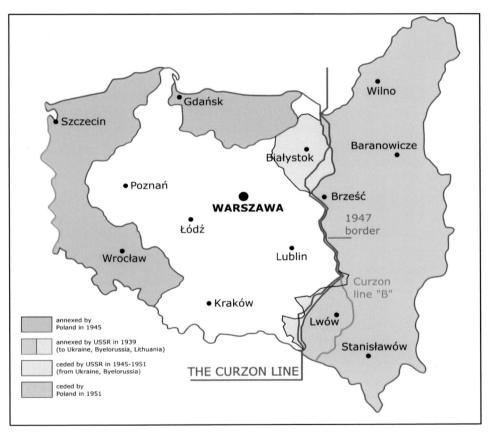

43 Map showing the Revised Polish Borders agreed by the three major powers at the Potsdam Conference in July 1945

The British objections were two-fold: the area in question was inhabited by between eight and ten million Germans – far too large to be handed over to Poland, and if the numbers involved were driven westwards it would impose an enormous burden on the occupying powers in the remainder of Germany.[145]

Stalin had the last word stating 'that we are confronted by a practical situation which admits to no other solution than to recognize the *fait accompli.*' [146]

Accordingly, the three major powers at the Conference agreed, as shown in the map above, that:

> *Pending the final determination of Poland's western frontier,*[147] *the former German territories east of a line running from the Baltic Sea along the Oder River to the confluence of the western Neisse River and along the western Neisse to the Czechoslovak frontier…shall be under the administration of the Polish State*

Other decisions determined at Potsdam in relation to Poland included the following:

> *Polish Provisional Government as the recognized government of the Polish State;*
>
> *To facilitate the return to Poland as soon as practicable of all Poles abroad who wish to go, including members of the Polish Armed Forces and the Merchant Marine;*
>
> *The expectation that those Poles who return home shall be accorded personal and property rights on the same basis as all Polish citizens;*
>
> *To note that the Polish Provisional Government has agreed to the holding of free and unfettered elections as soon as possible;*[148]
>
> *Having considered the question in all its aspects, recognition that the transfer of German populations, or elements thereof, remaining in*

Poland, Czechoslovakia and Hungary, will have to be undertaken.

Agreement that any transfers that take place should be effected in an orderly and humane manner.[149]

The recognition of the Polish Provisional Government as the recognized government of the Polish State by the United Kingdom and the USA resulted in the withdrawal of recognition from the Polish Government in Exile by the British Government. As a consequence, it had to give-up its headquarters at the Polish Embassy, in Portland Square, and withdraw to the Polish President's House at 43 Eaton Place, where it remained until 1990 functioning under extremely difficult circumstances, but in the knowledge that it remained the legitimate Government of Poland.

A further manifestation of the new order came in the debacle in June 1946 concerning the Victory Parade held in London when despite the role played by over 200,000 members of the Polish Armed Forces, there was no Polish representation.

The prevailing view is that the British Government wished to appease the Soviets by not inviting representatives of the Polish Forces, who were loyal to the Government in Exile and by definition opposed to the soviet controlled communist puppet government in Poland. Some have sought to down-play the matter and suggested that it was a straight forward administrative error and that the invitation was somehow sent in error to the government in Poland, but who declined the invitation.[150] That of course is a nonsense. At best it represented a total lack of sensitivity, and at worst political expediency. The resultant and very public controversy resulted in the matter being raised in Parliament,[151] where the level of offence that had been caused was at least recognised, but even last-minute invitations sent out in an attempt to expedite matters did little to resolve the issue. The affront to the Polish war effort has

107

never been forgotten, and the concession to the communist regime in Poland taken as a sign of things to come.

It was in the light of all these developments that in 1946, the 250,000 Poles still in uniform, including 110,000 in the Polish II Corps based in Italy, had to decide whether to return to Poland or seek a life in political exile

On 26 March, 1946, the British Foreign Secretary, Ernest Bevin, made a statement in parliament directed to the members of the Polish forces recommending to them, in the strongest possible terms, that they should return to Poland to help in the country's reconstruction,[152] some 105,000 did just that but some 123,000 did not. Why did so many Poles feel unable to return to Poland after the war? Mark Ostrowski cites three possible considerations,[153] but so much depended on individual circumstances.

In the case of Ludwik matters that would have affected his decision-making process may be summarised as follows:

Reasons to Return to Poland	*Reasons Not to Return to Poland*
As Ernest Bevin, the British Foreign Secretary put it, "… you should return to her [Poland] now, when she requires the help of all her sons in the arduous task of reconstructing the country and making good the devastation caused by the war".[154] Re-connecting with what was left of distant members of the family	*A tacit vote of confidence in the new communist regime, and a breach of trust in the cause of a democratic and independent Poland.* *Previous dealings with the Soviets:* *NKVD - the execution of his father Franciszek in 1940;* *Red Army - forcible deportation of him and his family to Kazakhstan in 1940;*

Onufry 〉 Franciszek 〉 Ludwik 〉 Franciszek 〉 **Ludwik** 〉 Ryszard

Reasons to Settle in England The Polish Resettlement Corps (Polski Korpus Przysposobienia i Rozmieszczenia) was established in May 1946 to provide Polish servicemen the opportunity for retraining and education. To live under a democratically elected government. The provision of a safe environment, accommodation, health, welfare provision and the prospect of employment, together with a network provided by fellow Poles arriving in identical circumstances. **Reasons not to Settle in England** A life in political exile. Post-war austerity. Learning a new language, and adapting to a new culture.	*The repressive Soviet backed communist Polish 'puppet' government;* *As the son of a serving police officer and land-owner he would be considered a 'class enemy' to Communism.* *The country had been devastated and left in ruins, first by the Germans and then the 'liberating' Red Army.* *There was no home to return to as both his father's former family homes were situated east of the Curzon-Line:* *Ruda Jaworska was now in Soviet Belarus and Folwark Han – the former family estate had been confiscated by the Soviets;* *The former family home in Cebrów was now in Soviet Ukraine.* *The prospect of becoming a Soviet citizen was a complete anathema.* *The prospect of starting a 'new life' in Upper Silesia or East Prussia in the territory that had been 'recovered' from Germany was ill-defined and full of uncertainty.* *Responsibility for the welfare and wellbeing of his siblings, Czesiek, Roman, and Teresa was of paramount importance.*

Assessing the issues highlighted above it is not difficult to see why Ludwik chose to settle in England, what is a little more difficult to comprehend is why over 42% of Poles, some 105,000 in total, chose to return to Poland, and even more so why a small minority were prepared to return to their homes in eastern Poland and live as Soviet citizens.

Notwithstanding the words of Bevin on 26 March 1946, there was a rapid turnabout by the British Government because on 22 May 1946, Bevin made a further statement to Parliament:

> *"As for those Poles who do not wish to return to Poland, it is our aim to demobilise them as quickly as possible and to arrange for their settlement in civilian life, either in Great Britain or overseas. Those serving abroad will be brought back to this, country, starting with those in Italy. Since it would be both impracticable and unfair to these gallant men, many of whom do not know our language, to launch them wholesale upon the labour market here and leave them to their own resources, His Majesty's Government are going to enrol them into a specially created Resettlement Corps...*
>
> *...essentially a transitional arrangement, designed to facilitate the transition from military to civil life. They will therefore be discharged from the Polish Armed Forces and enrolled in the Resettlement Corps with a view to their transfer to civilian life as soon as this becomes possible... As soon as settlement is complete the Corps will cease to exist.*
>
> *As a first step to demobilisation and the formation of the Resettlement Corps, His Majesty's Government have decided to bring the Polish 2nd Corps from Italy to the United*

*Kingdom. It is our intention to move their families
from Italy to the United Kingdom as soon as
administrative arrangements can be made."*[155]

The decision to form the Polish Resettlement Corps (PRC)
(Polski Korpus Przysposobienia i Rozmieszczenia) was followed
by what can best be described as a piece of enlightened and
magnanimous legislation. In April the Polish Resettlement Act
1947 was passed by Parliament. The Act was aimed specifically
at the needs of those who, were not prepared to return to
Poland, and were now identified and accepted by the British
Government as political refugees. The Act provided an
entitlement to the right to work, unemployment benefit, as well
as the provision of temporary accommodation in camps or
other establishments, together with access to health, and
educational services, for the former servicemen and their
dependents.[156] There is no doubt that provisions of the Act
enabled Poles to integrate into British society and contribute
to the economy far more easily and quickly than would
otherwise been possible. The following year provision was
made for Polish ex-servicemen to apply for British
Nationality,[157] a right that was subsequently incorporated in
the British Nationality Act of 1948.

Former army, and air force camps were used as Polish
Resettlement Camps (PRC) to provide temporary
accommodation for the Polish troops, and their families. By
October 1946, it is estimated that some 120,000 Polish troops
had been quartered in 265 camps throughout the United
Kingdom.[158] Following the 1951 census it is estimated that
there were 162,339 Polish-born residents in Britain compared
with 44,462 in 1931.[159]

Enrolment in the PRC was entirely voluntary, and for a
maximum period of two years, during which the servicemen
were accommodated in military camps, and paid the same rate
as regular members of the British Armed Forces.

The first recruits enrolled in September 1946, and as the aim was to enable and encourage access to full-time employment if, during the two years, a serviceman found employment they were demobilised and served the balance of the two-year period as a "Class W(T) Reserve".[160]

Ludwik finished his Pre-Officer Cadet Training Course (OCTU) at Matino in May 1946, and arrived in England with the rest of the II Corps in September. He was initially stationed at a temporary base established in the grounds of Sudbrooke Park in Lincolnshire. In December 1946 he joined the PRC, and was sent to the Liceum (Senior High School) that had been set up by the Polish Government in Exile in the grounds of Cannon Hall, in Cawthorne, near Barnsley, where he completed the 1st Year of the Advanced two-year in course Physics and Chemistry. As soon as Ludwik reached the age of twenty-one in June 1947, he was able to apply for his siblings, Czesiek, Roman, and Teresa, as his dependents, to be relocated from the Lebanon to England. Roman and Teresa arrived in Southampton on the *SS Chitral* at Southampton on 15 September 1947; listed in the ship's manifest as Passenger #250 Roman - Age 14 Student, and #251 Teresa - Age 8 Child.

Roman and Teresa, were accommodated at the Polish Displaced Persons Camp, in the former RAF Rivenhall, near Kelvedon in Essex, known colloquially by its residents as the "Obóz".[161] Their arrival coincided with the school at Cawthorne being permanently closed in October 1947. Ludwik, having just taken on the responsibilities for his siblings, decided not to transfer to the alternative Liceum at Riddlesworth Camp, in the grounds of Riddlesworth Park,[162] near Thetford, but instead took the option to be demobilised on 23 October 1947, and the following day was assigned to the Royal Army Reserve - Class 'W' until 12 December 1948.

Demobilsation meant that Ludwik had to register with the local authorities as a foreign 'Alien', and every time he either moved house or job had to register the fact with the local police. This draconian procedure continued until Ludwik finally applied for 'naturalisation' and became a British citizen in June 1960 – as did my mother, Czesia.

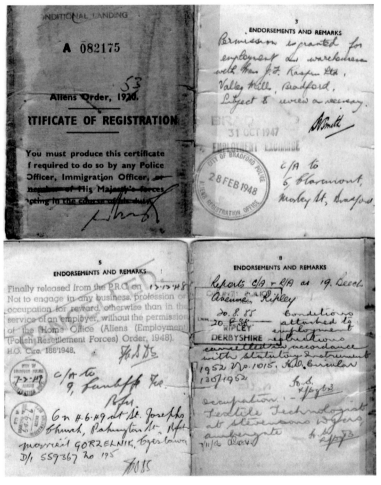

44 Pages from Ludwik Gan's Aliens' Certificate of Registration
1947 - 1960

Ludwik quickly found employment in the textile trade in nearby Bradford, starting on 31 October 1947, initially as a Warehouseman, then progressing to become a Backwasher Minder[163], and ultimately a Wool Comber[164], at JF Raspin Ltd. It meant that having found suitable accommodation he was

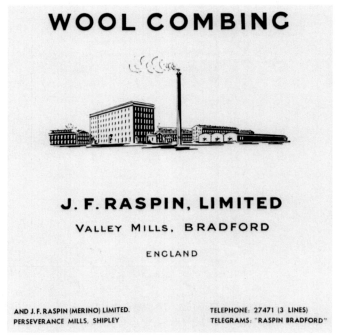

able to have Roman, Teresa and in due course Czesiek join him in Bradford.[165] My mother Czesia, meanwhile had been sponsored to come to England as the sole dependent of my uncle Józef, who had by 1947 completed his apprenticeship at RAF Halton and reached the age of twenty-one. Józef also

45 J.F. Raspin - the firm ceased trading in 1978

took the opportunity of anglicising his name from Gorzelnik[166] to Joseph Granville. Having arrived in England in November 1947, Czesia was housed at RAF Melton Mowbray, where Joseph was stationed at the time. She had travelled to England with two school friends, sisters Władisława, and Zofia Kukielke, who through a mutual contact had obtained employment in Shipley, near Bradford. They in turn recommended Czesia, which is why in March 1948 she accepted the offer of a job at a mill owned by C.F. Taylor and Co., on a wage of £3. 2s. 1d. (£114 in today's money -itm) for a five day-week, with an 11-hour day. The job came with board

Onufry ⟩ Franciszek ⟩ Ludwik ⟩ Franciszek ⟩ **Ludwik** ⟩ Ryszard

and lodgings in the women's' only hostel owned by the mill. Czesia's letter of appointment, states that the accommodation is centrally heated with hot and cold water in every room, at a rate of £1. 5s. (£46 itm) a week including: all meals, linen, and towels. Ludwik and Czesia first met in Bradford at a dance on New Year's Eve in 1948, both then became involved in helping run the Polish Library in Bradford on a voluntary basis. They married on 4 June 1949, spent a short honeymoon in Whitby, and their first son, named Ryszard Ludwik was born on 11 March 1950. [167]

46 Family Portrait - Bradford - March 1951
three generations of the Gan family safe in England
Czesia, Richard, Teresa
Czesiek, Ludwik, Great Uncle Józef, Roman

The responsibility of marriage and a first child spurred Ludwik to further his education. Having taken to the world of textiles he applied for and was accepted on a four-year Textile Diploma Course at Nottingham Technology College, with a student grant, starting in September 1951, and whilst still a student his second son Michael was born on 21 May 1953. After successfully gaining his Diploma, Ludwik took a job as an Assistant Manager with William Gibson's, a hosiery firm in Nottingham, before securing a position in 1955 more befitting of his qualifications, as the Manager of the Physical Testing Laboratory, at Stevensons' Dyers at Ambergate, near Ripley in Derbyshire. A long-standing family firm that had been established in 1893, it was generous to its employees, and with the job came the opportunity to rent a company house in Ripley. Since their arrival in England, they had always lived in multi-occupation premises, and so the house in Beech Avenue was the first family home they had to themselves, and where they spent eight happy years, interrupted by a horrific and life-threatening car crash that Ludwik suffered as a passenger in October 1956. It took him almost twelve months to fully recover, from major head and facial injuries, and was one reason why he never obtained a driving licence. Up to that time Ludwik had been quite active in various Polish political groups in England, but the effect of the accident and pressure of work meant that it gradually diminished. Whilst at Stevensons, Ludwik invented and patented the Dylan Cubex – a piece

47 Ludwik Gan - 1966

of equipment designed to for the control testing of shrink resistance in wool, and whilst it made his name in the world of textiles it did not bring any financial reward. The family was eventually able to buy its first, and indeed only home, when it

Onufry 〉 Franciszek 〉 Ludwik 〉 Franciszek 〉 **Ludwik** 〉 Ryszard

moved to Tollerton in 1965. That previous year Ludwik started lecturing part-time in textiles at what was then Nottingham Regional College, now Trent University. From there it was a natural move for him to be appointed in 1969 to a full-time lectureship at Leicester Polytechnic, now de Montfort University, with promotion to Senior Lecturer coming the following year. In addition to a full teaching programme, during his time at Leicester, he took full advantage of the opportunity to continue with his research, publish over twenty-one technical papers, and accept invitations to address some seven conferences - including four overseas. He also found time to further his own studies and in 1978 was awarded an MPhil from Leeds University. The subject of his thesis was *'Dimensional Behaviour during Relaxation of Weft-Knitted Structures containing Tuck Stitches'* - a subject that is unlikely to be meaningful to the majority of readers – not least myself. Ludwik retired from the Polytechnic in 1990, and was able to devote more time to his hobby of photography, but his final years were blighted by the onset of Alzheimer's Disease from which he died in 2011 at the age of 85.

If there was any doubt in Ludwik's mind as to whether he had made the right decision of not returning to Poland after the War, they must have been few and far between. As early as March 1946 Churchill had raised the sceptre of an 'iron curtain' descending across Europe, with Communist parties being raised to pre-eminence and power far beyond their numbers and seeking everywhere to obtain totalitarian control, with Police governments prevailing in nearly every case.[168] The 'cold-war' was long-lasting, for example the War Office only became the Department of Defence as late as 1964. He would have been the first to readily acknowledge the outstanding achievement of the Polish people in the reconstruction of Poland following its almost complete devastation during the war, despite the burden of the suppression under the yoke of Communism.

1989 saw the first free-elections held in Poland and the election of a democratic non-communist government. If Ludwik had any lingering doubts they would have been finally dispelled in December 1990, when the President of Polish Government in Exile, Ryszard Kaczorowski, formally transferred his authority to the newly elected President of Poland, Lech Wałęsa. He symbolically did so by handing over the seals of state of the Polish Republic, together with the presidential seal, the presidential banner, and a copy of the original text of the Polish Constitution of 1935, under which the Government in Exile had been acting since 1939.[169] The Polish White Eagle was again wearing its crown after an absence of nearly forty-five years.

48 The Crowned White Eagle the symbol of Polish sovereign independence

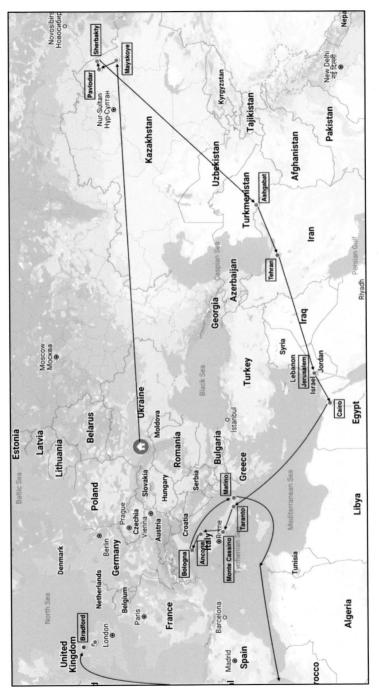

49 Map showing the 10,500-mile journey undertaken by Ludwik Gan 1940 - 1946

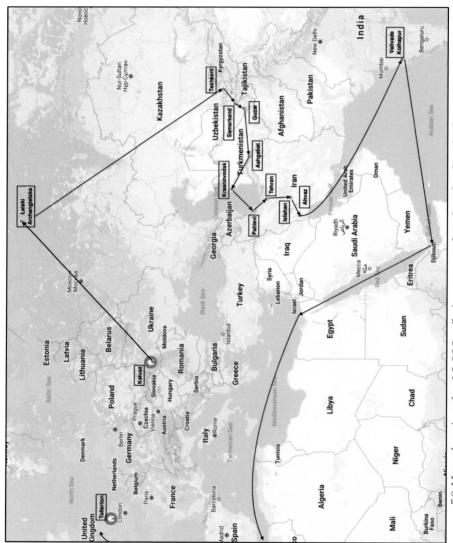

50 Map showing the 16,000-mile journey undertaken by Czesia Gan 1940 -1946

Polish-Yorkshireman

1950 –

According to John Keegan the "the new generation of Poles, through the dedication and self-sacrifice of their parents, have become the most successful immigrant community ever absorbed into British life"[170]

Ryszard Ludwik Gan[171] - but always known as Richard, except at home - was born on 11 March 1950, in Bradford, Yorkshire. The following year his parents Ludwik, and Czesia moved to Nottingham, where Ludwik had a place to study for a Diploma in Textile at the College of Technology. Richard's first language was Polish, and he did not speak any English until he started, aged five, at the nearby Sacred Heart Convent School. In later years his mother would continue to speak to him in Polish whilst he responded in English. Having gained his Diploma, Ludwik secured a position with Stevensons Dyers in Ambergate, and so the family moved to nearby Ripley in Derbyshire. Richard, and subsequently his brother Michael, attended the Catholic Primary school, St. Elizabeth's Convent School at Belper, some six miles away. Richard and Michael were accompanied to and from the nearby bus stop every day by Czesia, for the relatively short bus journey. Czesia and Ludwik had previously decided that Ludwik's career would take precedence and that Czesia would remain at home to look after the children and maintain the house; an arrangement that proved most beneficial and effective. However, one downside was that with only one income coming into the house, money was always tight – whilst not poor by any stretch of the imagination – it did mean careful budgeting, with relatively few luxuries, and no prospect of foreign holidays, or overseas school trips.

In 1961 Richard successfully passed his 11+ scholarship exam but having been offered a place at Swanwick Grammar School, it was decided that he should go to The Becket School,[172] an independent Catholic Direct Grant Grammar School,[173] situated in West Bridgford, a suburb of Nottingham, a long stone's throw from the famous Trent Bridge. The journey of some fifteen miles took one and a half hours each way, requiring two buses with a good walk at either end. It was a long day, with the morning bus leaving at 7.00 a.m. – but one advantage of the long journey time was that Richard was often able to complete his homework on the bus on the return journey.

He graduated from London University, Chelsea College,[174] with an honours degree in Geology in 1972, which he followed by a one-year, Post Graduate Certificate in Education at the Institute of Education[175], where he combined getting a double-distinction whilst at the same time serving as President of the Students' Union. He married for the first time, whilst still a student, and was living in Twickenham, when in 1973 he secured a science teaching post at Raynes Park High School, in South West London. During his two years at the school he studied part-time, again at Chelsea, for a Master's degree in Education. Having finished his part-time higher degree, in order to widen his experience, Richard took on some part-time lecturing in the Earth Sciences with the Open University. One of the perks of the job was exemption from tuition-fees, which is how it came about that, having studied - again part-time - he was awarded a BA in Management Studies by the Open University in 1980.

Rapid promotion in his teaching career came in 1977, when having spent two years as Deputy Head of Science at Featherstone High School in Southall, he was appointed as Head of the Science Faculty at Shene School in Richmond. Having decided that management rather than teaching was his forte, in 1979 he joined the local government sector as an education administrator. His first appointment was with the London Borough of Hounslow (Labour controlled), followed by the L.B. of Waltham Forest (Conservative controlled), anfinally, in 1986 as Assistant Director of Education, and Head of the Schools Division with the Royal Borough of Kingston-Upon-Thames (Initially Liberal, and subsequently Conservative controlled). By 1992 he had tired of the politics, budget reductions, and the seemingly endless round of late-night meetings; and found greater job-satisfaction in taking on the role as Bursar and Clerk to the Governing Body at the London Nautical School. Wondering why his predecessor had left so quickly he soon found the answer – a projected deficit of £130,000 compared with the surplus of £35,000 the Governors had been led to believe. However, by the end of the following financial year, having put in place new budget procedures and with careful monitoring, he managed to turn the deficit into a surplus of £130,000.

Richard had become a Freemason in 1977 in Nottingham having been proposed by his then father-in-law, Lewis Winter an enthusiastic and locally well-known and respected Freemason. Unsurprisingly, given where he was living, most of Richard's Masonic activities took place in Middlesex and London. Management being his strength, he soon became involved as the secretary of his various units, and from there became a successful and well-known provincial administrator. Almost without exception, all the various roles within Freemasonry are carried out on a completely voluntary basis. At headquarters level there are at best two or three high level professionally paid jobs, and as might be expected vacancies occur only once or twice in a generation. In 1996, the position of Grand Secretary of the Grand Lodge of Mark Master Masons (GLMMM) based in St. James's, London did fall vacant, and Richard applied for the post. In the ordinary course of events, one does not get a cigar for coming second, but on this occasion, having failed to get the top-job, he was offered and accepted the post of Assistant Grand Secretary. In 1995, Richard, having divorced his previous wife, married Niki, at that time Deputy Head of Newland House Preparatory School, subsequently Head of Blackheath High Junior School, and ultimately Rupert House Preparatory School in Henley-on-

Thames. She would often joke that whilst Richard went off to 'hobby' she would go off to actual work. The privilege of being paid for enjoying one's hobby cannot be overstated, and Richard took to it like a duck to water. A position that he would have gladly undertaken for no remuneration. It gave him the opportunity to not only make a substantial and worthwhile contribution to Freemasonry, but also the chance to travel extensively both at home and abroad, and in the process make friends throughout the world.

Having been promoted as Deputy Grand Secretary in 2005, the highlight of his career was probably his organisation of the celebrations of the sesquicentenary of Mark Masonry[176] in 2006, with a dinner for five-hundred guests in the historic Great Hall in Guildhall in the City of London. This was followed

51 Richard Gan - 2010

next day by a celebratory meeting for 5,500 Masons and their wives, at the Royal Albert Hall, attended by the Grand Master of the Mark, HRH Prince Michael of Kent, HRH Princess Michael of Kent, HRH The Duke of Kent, and in her capacity as Patron of the National Osteoporosis Society, HRH the Duchess of Cornwall, who during the ceremony was presented with a donation to the Society for £3 million pounds.

Onufry 〉 Franciszek 〉 Ludwik 〉 Franciszek 〉 Ludwik 〉 **Ryszard**

Retirement from full-time employment in June 2010, gave Richard the opportunity to take a greater interest in Masonic research and writing. From 2010 until 2014 he was the Editor of *The Square,* an independent magazine published by Lewis Masonic the world's oldest Masonic publisher. Whilst under his editorship the magazine was aimed at a readership that was not exclusively Masonic and carried a wide range of articles that were predominantly historical in nature.

Relinquishing the role of Editor in 2014 gave Richard even more time as an independent scholar to develop his own writing and research into Victorian Freemasonry, and the Progressive Masonic Orders in particular. He has had three books published, together with four monographs, four essays, and two papers based on original research using primary sources. In addition to the publications, he has given over twenty-two formal lectures and talks on a range of Masonic subjects, in England and overseas.

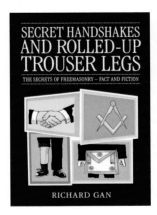 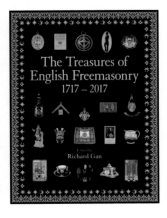 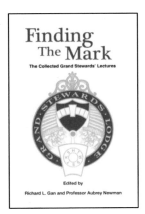

52 Richard Gan's three published books

In addition to his membership of many Masonic units, Richard has for many years enjoyed a varied and extensive range of interests and activities including: playing sport at club level: lawn tennis, squash, golf, croquet and bowls; watching football, and cricket; membership of various clubs and societies including the Marylebone Cricket Club (MCC), and Glyndebourne Festival Society; being granted the Freedom of the City of London, and becoming a Liveryman; a Knight Commander of the Order of St. Lazarus of Jerusalem;[177] Photography, the results of which decorate his home, though it has to be added, restricted mostly to his study; a Presiding Magistrate for some eighteen years - pro. bono., and on reaching the statutory retirement age in 2020, placed on the Supplemental List, enabling him to continue to use the letters J.P. after his name.[178]

At the time of his retirement from full-time work Richard and his delightful, and supportive wife Niki were living in Henley on Thames. When Niki decided to take early-retirement in 2013, after seven very successful years as the Headmistress at Rupert House Prep. School, and not having any ties to the area, they decided to move to rural Lincolnshire. The move enabled them to enjoy a more relaxed life-style, and take a more active part in the local community. In addition, the excellent road network, and a train journey to London that only takes an hour and a half – door to door – meant that Richard could still continue with his Masonic activities in London.

A Polish citizen from birth, Richard was always proud of his Polish heritage. Satisfied that Poland was now an independent, democratic sovereign state, he finally decided to apply for a passport - the ultimate proof of his citizenship. The process took well over a year involving the completion - in Polish - of numerous forms, obtaining the necessary documentary evidence, providing copies of certified translations, and several visits to the Polish Consulate in both Manchester and London, but finally Richard, or rather Ryszard, was issued with his Polish Passport in December 2019.

Polish-Yorkshireman
Onufry 〉 Franciszek 〉 Ludwik 〉 Franciszek 〉 Ludwik 〉 **Ryszard**

53 Richard Gan's Polish Passport

Epilogue

To be successful as an immigrant or indeed the child of an immigrant one needs fully to accept and respect the ethos and values of the adopted country, there can be no half-way house. That is not the same as saying that one needs to abandon the cultural heritage of one's homeland, as has been proven by such famous Polish exiles as Mickiewicz, and Chopin. Whilst in no way wishing to be drawn into any comparison with their undoubted eminence and merit, the commonality is straight forward - being Polish is an intellectual concept that is not bound by territorial boundaries. A fact amply confirmed time and time again throughout the history of Poland. Hence it is perfectly normal in being described as a Polish-Yorkshireman, and taking great pride in being both at the same time.

The term successful is highly subjective. Has, for example, the branch of the family that came and settled in England been more successful than those that remained in Poland – who can tell? The best I can proffer from a personal point of view is encompassed in that wonderful French expression – *bien dans sa peau*. Not easy to translate the nuance into either English or Polish, but in essence *being content or comfortable in one's own skin* – in Polish - *dobre uczucie*, that I believe is the closest one is likely to get in deciding whether or not one has been successful.

I believe that it is not tautological to attempt to differentiate between a history of the Gan family as opposed to a Gan family history. A family history, more often than not concentrates on creation of a family tree, the presentation of dates of birth, death and marriage and, where sufficient information is available, perhaps a short pen-picture on individual members. I however have endeavoured to provide a history of the Gan family in the widest sense, albeit with the focus on my own branch, by concentrating on a limited number of individuals to whom I am directly related, and setting it into the context of nearly five-hundred years of Polish history.

My sincere wish is that other, especially younger members of the family, will take some encouragement from this work in progress and take the opportunity to research further into their own branch of the family. There is now a considerable amount of digital information available world-wide, which makes the task somewhat easier, but they should not make the same mistake as myself, in leaving it almost too late. The death of members of the family, meant that one very important avenue of obtaining first-hand information was closed for ever and which, undoubtedly, made the task that much more difficult. I look forward to reading companion volumes to this book in the years to come.

The members of the Gan family have much to be proud about, having successfully survived the vagaries of history for nearly five hundred years. There is nothing to suggest that it will not survive for a further five-hundred years, providing they continue to adapt to circumstances, usually beyond their control, and remain proud of and never forget their Polish roots and heritage.

Appendix 1

Franciszek Gan's - Military Decorations and Regimental Commemorative Badges

Medal Pamiątkowy za Wojnę 1918–1921
(Commemorative Medal for the War of 1918 – 1921)

Established in September 1928 and awarded to soldiers who fought for Polish Independence between November 1918 and March 1921.

54 Medal Pamiątkowy za Wojnę 1918–1921

A round medal with a diameter of 35 mm, made of brass and suspended from a ribbon 37mm in width, that reflect the colours of the Order of the Virtuti Militari, and the Cross of Valour.

On the obverse is the Polish white eagle wearing a crown, on its chest is the cross of the order of military Virtuti Militari. On either side of its claws are the dates: 1918 and 1921.

On the reverse is a wreath of oak leaves, inside which is the inscription: Polska Swemu Obrońcy *(Poland His Defender)*.

Medal Dziesięciolecia Odzyskanej Niepodległości
(Medal of the Decade of Regained Independence)

Awarded to personnel who, for a minimum period of five years, between November 1918 and 1928, gave impeccable service in the Police, military and other public services.

55 Medal Dziesięciolecia Odzyskanej Niepodległośc

Appendix 1 - Franciszek Gan's - Military Decorations and Regimental Commemorative Badges

A round medal with a diameter of 35 mm, made of bronze suspended on the light-blue ribbon 38 mm in width.

On the obverse is the profile of the head of the Marshal Józef Piłsudski.

On the reverse the dates: 1918-1928 and the image of a ploughman with a plough removing thistles to symbolize the work of starting from scratch.

Regimental Commemorative Badges

5 Pułk Ułanów Kaniowskich, 6 puł
6th Kaniow Ułan (Light Cavalry) Regiment

56 Regimental Badge – 5 Pułk Ułanów Kaniowskich, 6 puł
6th Kaniow Ułan (Light Cavalry) Regiment

A Maltese cross with arms enamelled in the blue of regimental pennants. On the horizontal arms of the cross, blue chevrons on a white stripe. In the centre of the cross a silver Jagiellonian eagle with a blue enamelled shield on its chest inscribed with the number and initial "6 U". The badge, measuring, 52x52 mm, was designed by Jan Knedler of Warsaw.

Szósty Pułk Artylerii Polowej
Sixth Field Artillery Regiment

57 Regimental Badge - Szósty Pułk Artylerii Polowej
Sixth Field Artillery Regiment

A dark green and black enamelled cross with bevelled arms. The number 6 and the initials PAP set in silver on the green enamelled arms of the cross. In the centre, of the cross, on a blue enamel background, both in silver, the coat of arms of the city of Kraków, surrounded by a laurel wreath. The crossed silver barrels of two cannon between the arms of the cross. The badge, measuring, 46x46 mm, was designed by Józef Trębacz of Kraków.

Appendix 2

Index of individuals included in the Extracts from the Family Tree with the Surname Gan *

Name	Date of Birth	Date of Marriage	Date of Death	Spouse
Agnieszka *Ledzioszek*	28/05/1965	17/09/1988		Robert
Alexander	05/06/1997			
Alojsy Herculan	1818			
Andrew J	1963	May 1994		Elizabeth Wright
Andrzej Piotr	c. 1664			
Andrzej Wazil	c. 1618	c. 1634	c. 1678	
Anna	c. 1815	1835	c. 1875	Jerzy Rogiński
Anna Katarzyna *Jatwott*	1865			Władysław
Anna-Małgorzata	c. 1620	c. 1640		Jan-Krzysztof Neuhof Von der Ley
Antoni	c. 1820	1846		Wiktoria Wojnicka
Antoni Franciszek	c. 1707		1767	
Antoni Jozef	c. 1730		1780	
Antoni Jozef	c. 1766	1802	1824	Katarzyna Symanowska
Antoni Kazimierz	c. 1746		1806	
Antonina	c. 1823	1843	c. 1883	Franciszek Lastowski
Antonia *Ćwirko*	1803			Jan Michał
Antonia *Korejwo*	1810			Kazimierz Jozef
Antonina *Michałowska*	1816			Jozef Michał
Arkadiusz	25/11/1995			

Gan – is that a Polish Name?

Name	Date of Birth	Date of Marriage	Date of Death	Spouse
Barbara *Czeknowska*	1859			Jerzy B
Barbara *Edgrid*	1778	1798	1828	Bartłomiej J
Barbara *Lewkowicz*	1786			Kazimierz Jozef
Bartłomiej J	c. 1760	1798		Barbara Edgrid
Bartłomiej Jakub	c. 1700		c. 1760	
Bartłomiej JM	c. 1817	c. 1838	c. 1902	Marianna
Beata				Grzegorz Głowacki
Beata *??*	17/09/1969	20/04/1996		Robert Maciej
Bogdan	1940			Regina *??*
Boniface Jozef	c. 1704		c. 1764	
Bożena *Kosior*	19/05/1955			Mirosław
Cecylia *Bortkiewicz*	1835			Tomasz Jakub
Cezara				Eugeniusz Kędra
Czeslaw Felicjan	07/10/1929	10/08/1960	01/07/1984	Herma Fromwald
Czesława *Gorzelnik*	01/11/1928	06/06/1949		Ludwik Romuald
Damian	27/03/1987			
Daniel	12/08/1988			
Daniel Michael	c. 1728	1782	c. 1788	
Dominik Jozef	c. 1702		c. 1762	
Dorota *??*				Ignacy
Dorota *Widuch*	09/04/1967	28/04/1990		Edward
Edward	13/08/1967	28/04/1990		Dorota Widuch

Appendix 2: Index of individuals included in the Extracts from the Family Tree with the Surname Gan *

Name	Date of Birth	Date of Marriage	Date of Death	Spouse
Edward Marek	13/10/1959	31/01/1987		Jadwiga Wodzińska
Elizabeth *Winter*	16/12/1950	01/01/1971		Richard
Elizabeth *Wright*	01/05/1994			Andrew J
Elżbieta	c. 1860		1876	
Emil	1937			Emilia *??*
Emilia *??*				Emil
Emilia *Uklewska*				Franciszek Kazimierz
Eugeniusz				*Stanisława Kobylarz*
Felican Michael	c. 1720		c. 1780	
Feliks	12/2/1890	12/03/1971		Helena *??*
Filomena *Czuczejko*		1905		Ludwik Franciszek
Fortunat Karol	1821			
Francis Michael	1961	1994		Patricia W McCrae
Franciszek Ludwik	10/03/1899	1940		Michalina Izewska
Franciszek Kazimierz	1819		c. 1883	Emilia Uklewska
Franciszek Kazimierz	c. 1751		1811	
Franciszek Piotr	c. 1659		c. 1735	
Genowefa *Wojtuszko*	1905	1996		Józef Ludwik
Grażyna *Kopiec*	1954	1974		Michael
Helena *??*	12/12/1903	12/03/1975		Feliks
Herma *Fromwald*		10/8/1960		Czesław Felicjan
Hieronim Daniel	c. 1762		c. 1822	

Gan – is that a Polish Name?

Name	Date of Birth	Date of Marriage	Date of Death	Spouse
Hieronim Jozef	1843		c. 1903	
Ignacy	c. 1772	c. 1790	c. 1850	Dorota ??
Ignacy Daniel	c. 1760		c. 1820	
Irena				Jan Leptuch
Jadwiga *Wodzińska*	13/08/1964	31/01/1987		Edward Marek
Jakub	10/03/1993			
Jakub	c. 1733			
Jakub Jerzy	c. 1745		1805	
Jakub Piotr	c. 1668		c. 1728	
Jan		1915		
Jan Jozef	c. 1700		1775	
Jan Michał	c. 1769	1803	1823	Antonia Ćwirko
Jan Piotr	c. 1666			
Jerzy Antoni	c. 1747		1807	
Jerzy Franciszek	c. 1700		1771	
Jerzy Kazimierz	c. 1747		1807	
Maciej	c. 1530	c. 1561	c. 1600	
Jerzy Maciej	c. 1580	c. 1599	c. 1640	
Jerzy Mikolai	c. 1851		c. 1911	
Jerzy Paweł	c. 1706		c. 1766	
Jerzy Teofil	c. 1672		c. 1732	
Jerzy B	c. 1839	1859	c. 1889	Barbara Czeknowska
Jozef	c. 1730		c. 1793	
Jozef Daniel	c. 1758		c. 1818	

Appendix 2: Index of individuals included in the Extracts from the Family Tree with the Surname Gan *

Name	Date of Birth	Date of Marriage	Date of Death	Spouse
Jozef Jakub	c. 1702		c. 1762	
Jozef Jerzy	c. 1738		1798	
Józef Ludwik	05/05/1897	17/10/1963		Genowefa Wojtuszko
Jozef Michał	c. 1779	c. 1840	c. 1850	Ludwika Michałowska
Jozef Mikołaj	c. 1725		c. 1785	
Jozef Piotr	c. 1670	c. 1725	c. 1757	Marcjanna
Jozef Teofil	c. 1674		c. 1734	
Józefa		1828		
Józefa				?? Dojlid
Jozefa *Bogdaszewska*	1897			Julius Tomasz
Julia	03/05/1973			David Gallimore
Julius Tomasz	c. 1867	1897		Jozefa Bogdaszewska
Justin Michael	c. 1726		c. 1786	
Justyna *Okulewicz*	1816			Stanisław Jerzy
Kajetan Michael	c. 1722		c. 1786	
Karol Adolf	1818			
Karolina	1826	1846		Jozef Szczepanowicz
Karolina *Tomaszewska*	1816			Tomasz Jakub
Katarzyna *Kierbedz*	1797			Stanisław Jerzy
Katarzyna *Symanowska*	c. 1782	1802		Antoni Jozef
Kazimiera	c. 1768		1828	
Kazimiera *Bolesława*	1847		c. 1907	
Kazimierz	c. 1759			

139

Gan – is that a Polish Name?

Name	Date of Birth	Date of Marriage	Date of Death	Spouse
Kazimierz	c. 1819	1842	c. 1877	Zuzanna Ejgrida
Kazimierz Jakub	c. 1721		c. 1781	
Kazimierz Jozef	c. 1766	1786	c. 1826	Barbara Lewkowicz
Kazimierz Piotr	c. 1660		c. 1720	
Konstanty	1821		1874	Ludwika Łasko
Krystynia *Dmochowska*	c. 1786	1806	c. 1846	Tomasz Marcin
Lisa *??*				Andrew J
Ludwik Franciszek	02/04/1866		1923	Filomena Czuczejko
Ludwik Jakub	c. 1698		c. 1758	
Ludwik Romuald	21/06/1926	06/06/1949	11/07/2011	Czesława Gorzelnik
Ludwika *Łasko*				Konstanty
Ludwika *Michałowska*		c. 1840		Jozef Michał
Ludwika *Rushchtys*	c. 1831	1851	c. 1891	Mikolai
Maciej	16/01/1984	10/07/2010		Monika Wolska
Maciej Kazimierz	c. 1752			
Marcjanna *??*				Jozef Piotr
Marcin	c. 1730		c. 1790	
Margaret E *Wright*	06/08/1953	23/03/1996		Michael
Maria	1817			
Marianna *??*		c. 1838		Bartłomiej JM
Mariola	17/11/1960	April 1982		Marek Piekarski
Maryanna	c. 1640			

Appendix 2: Index of individuals included in the Extracts from the Family Tree with the Surname Gan *

Name	Date of Birth	Date of Marriage	Date of Death	Spouse
Matilda Michała *Ejgirda*	c. 1638	13/02/1658	1698	Piotr Andrzej
Michael	21/05/1953	23/03/1996		Margaret E Wright
Michał Antoni	c. 1739	1774	1799	Wiktoria Piotrowicz
Michał Kazimierz	c. 1691		c. 1751	
Michalina *Izewska*	20/09/1899	11/05/1942		Franciszek Ludwik
Mikolai	1807	1851	c. 1867	Ludwika Rushchtys
Mikołaj Kazimierz	c. 1690		c. 1750	
Milan	09/07/2012			
Mirosław	09/08/1953			Bożena Kosior
Monika *Wolska*	10/11/1983	10/07/2010		Maciej
Natalia	09/11/2000			
Niki *Collins*	08/01/1957	19/08/1995		Richard
Nina	18/04/1997			
Olimpia *Safianowicz*				Ludwik Franciszek
Onufry Stanisław	1777	1814	c. 1837	Katarzyna Giedrojć
Patricia W *McCrae*	1994			Francis Michael
Paweł Piotr	c. 1662			
Paweł Teofil	c. 1676		c. 1736	
Petronella *Kierbedź*	c. 1791	1804	1811	Onufry Stanisław
Piotr Andrzej	c. 1638	13/02/1658	c. 1695	Matilda Michała Ejgirda
Regina ??	13/04/1945		28/01/2011	Bogdan
Richard Ludwik	11/03/1950	19/08/1995		Niki Collins

Gan – is that a Polish Name?

Name	Date of Birth	Date of Marriage	Date of Death	Spouse
Robert	26/11/1963	17/09/1988		Agnieszka Ledzioszek
Robert Maciej	02/04/1969	20/04/1996		Beata ??
Roman	25/07/1933	26/10/1963	27/11/2003	Teresa Sierzputowska
Rozalia	c. 1816	1836		Jozef Romanowski
Stanisław Jan	c. 1790	1810	c. 1843	Wiktoria Komarowicz
Stanisław Jerzy	c. 1740		1799	Zofia ??
Stanisław Jerzy	c. 1777	1797	c. 1837	Katarzyna Kierbedź
Stanisław Tadeuz	c. 1753		1813	
Stanisława	07/07/1929		03/03/1998	Alfons Zabłocki
Stanisława *Kobylarz*				Eugeniusz
Tadeuz Jerzy	c. 1730		1790	
Teofil	c. 1642		c. 1698	
Teresa	c. 1816	1833	c. 1876	Franciszek Baranowicz
Teresa	19/01/1939	07/07/74		Eligiusz Eugeniusz Tomaszewski
Teresa *Sierzputowska*	13/4/1944	26/10/1963		Roman
Tomasz Jakub	c. 1769	1816	c. 1846	Karolina Tomaszewska
Tomasz Jerzy	c. 1742		c. 1831	
Tomasz Kazimierz	c. 1754		c. 1831	
Tomasz Marcin	1775	1806	1864	Krystynia Dmochowska
Tomasz Tomasz	1832		c. 1892	
Victoria	02/01/2001			
Wazil Jerzy	c. 1600		c. 1660	

Appendix 2: Index of individuals included in the Extracts from the Family Tree with the Surname Gan *

Name	Date of Birth	Date of Marriage	Date of Death	Spouse
Wiktoria *Komarowicz*	1810	1813		Stanisław Jan
Wiktoria *Marcinkiewicz*	1813			Stanisław Jan
Wiktoria *Piotrowicz*	c. 1754	1774	1813	Michał Antoni
Wiktoria *Wojnicka*	1846			Antoni
Wincenty Michał	c. 1724		c. 1784	
Wincenty Tadeuz	c. 1754		1829	
Wioletta *Ślugajska*				Marcin
Władysław	1836	1865	1876	Anna Katarzyna Jatwott
Władysław Alfons	1820			
Zofia *??*				Stanisław Jerzy
Zuzanna *Ejgrida*	c. 1822	1842	c. 1882	Kazimierz

* In order to avoid unnecessary repetition, if the Surname is Gan at birth only the first name is given:
i.e. Richard is Richard [Gan]
If the Surname became Gan on marriage then the maiden name follows the first name in italics:
i.e. Niki *Collins* took the name Niki Gan when she married Richard [Gan]
Where the maiden name is not known, it is shown as *??*
i.e. Dorota *??* took the name Dorota Gan when she married Ignacy [Gan]
Where a female member of the family born with the name Gan has married she is listed under her first name, and her married name can be deduced from that of her spouse
i.e. Teresa [Gan] when she married took the name Teresa Tomaszewski

Appendix 3

Family Tree of the Turczanski Branch of the Family

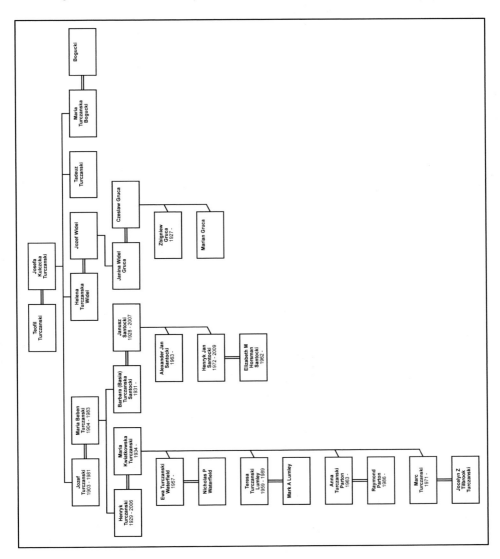

Gan – is that a Polish Name?

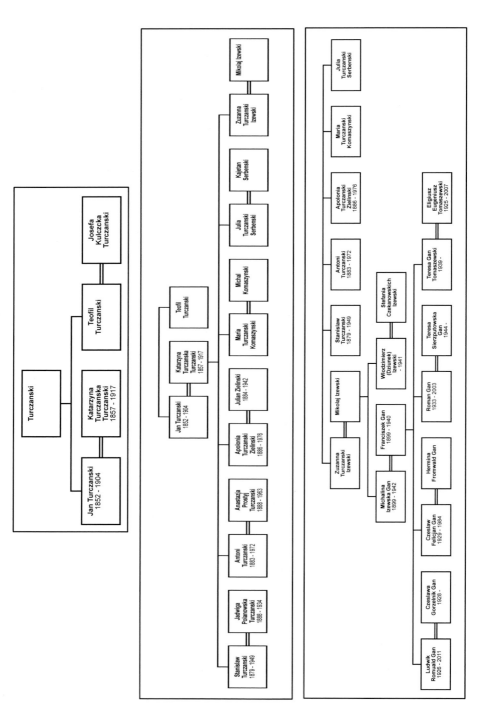

Family Tree of the Turczanski Branch of the Family

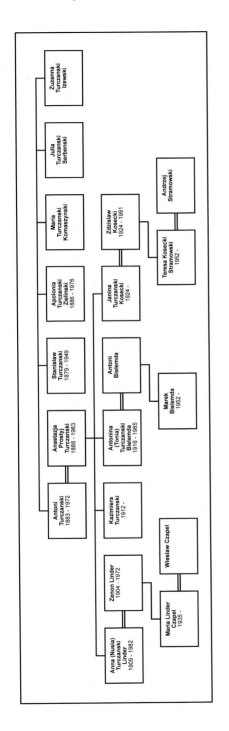

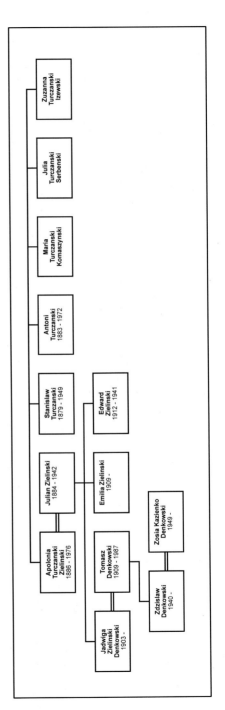

Bibliography

Bartov, Omer, *Anatomy of a Genocide: The Life and Death of a Town Called Buczacz*, Simon & Schuster, 2018,
ISBN 978 1 4516 8453 7

Collective Work, *Second World War Story Poles In India 1942-1948*, Association of Poles in India 1942-1948, 2000,
ISBN 978 0 9538928 2 2

Davies, Norman, *God's Playground: A History of Poland: Volume 1 The Origins to 1795*, Clarendon Press Oxford, 1981,
ISBN 0 19 821 943 1

Davies, Norman, *God's Playground: A History of Poland: Volume II 1795 to the Present*, Clarendon Press Oxford, 1981,
ISBN 0 19 821 944

Davies, Norman, *The Anders Army, An Odyssey Across Three Continents*, 2015, Osprey, pp530-531,
ISBN 9781472816030

Lukowski, Jerzy and Zawadski Hubert, *A Concise History of Poland*, Cambridge University Press, 2009,
ISBN 978 0 521 61857 1

Malewski Czesław, *Rodziny szlacheckie na Litwie w XIX wieku Powiaty lidzki, oszmiański i wileński,* Warszawa, 2016,
ISBN 978 83 63352 75 2

Snyder, Timothy, *The Reconstruction of Nations: Poland, Ukraine, Lithuania, Belarus*, 1569-1999, Yale, 2003,
ISBN 0 300 10586 x, p15

Zamoyski, Adam, *Poland A History*, Harper Press, 2009,
ISBN 978 0 00 728275 3

Notes

1   Czesław Malewski, *Rodziny Szlacheckie na Litwie w XIX wieku Powiaty Lidzki, Oszmiański i Wileński*, Warszawa, 2016.

2   Lithuanian State Historical Archives Vilnius, zesp. 391, inv. 1, Vol. 992, pp. 15 to 20 – 1799.

3   Lithuanian State Historical Archives Vilnius, zesp. 391, inv. 1, Vol. 1429, pp. 6 to 9 – 1811 in Polish.

4   Lithuanian State Historical Archives Vilnius, zesp. 391, inv. 1, Vol. 1429, pp. 346 to 349 – 1885 in Russian.

5   [Accessed 25 June 2020] <geneteka.genealodzy.pl/index.php?op=gt&lang=eng&bdm=S& w=22br&rid=S&search_lastname=gan&search_name=&search_ lastname2=&search_name2=&from_date=&to_date=&rpp1=&or dertable=>

6   In early Poland it was customary for names to consist of three elements: the first or given name (imię), a patronymic (patronimiczne), and a surname or family name (nazwisko). The patronymic is derived from the father's given name with the usually the addition of ...czyk or ...owicz for men; ...owna for married women, and ...ówna for maiden names. In more recent times the practice has been to add syn or s. (son of) after the family name. Thus Jerzy Maciejowicz – Jerzy son of Maciej; and Franciszek s. Ludwik – Franciszek son of Ludwik. The form used throughout the book depends on the source, but wherever possible the simplest or anglicised from of name is used, thus Jerzy Maciej, but where appropriate and if derived from official documents, Jerzy Maciejowicz, or Jerzy s. Maciej.

7   Eidintas Alfonsas, Bumblauskas Alfredas, Kulakauskas Antanas, Tamošaitis Mindaugas, Translated and Edited by Kondratas, Skirma and Kondratas, Ramūnas, *The History Of Lithuania*, 2015, ISBN 978 609 437 163 9, p142

8   Snyder, Timothy, *The Reconstruction of Nations: Poland, Ukraine, Lithuania, Belarus*, 1569-1999, Yale, 2003, ISBN 0 300 10586 x, p15.

9   The English equivalent of Folwark is a Grange Farm.

10   Bajer, Piotr Pawel, Polish Nobility and Its Heraldry: An Introduction, p11, podolska.neostrada.pl/teksty/heraldry.htm accessed 24 January 2020.

11   It should be noted that Poland did have a very small number of Princely families, either descended from the Royal Family or created by the Sejm [Polish Parliament].

12   Ennoblement by heraldic adoption was abolished by 1633.

13   In 1578 the king was deprived, by the Sejm - Plebeiorum Nobilitato - of his power to create new grants of ennoblement, other than for outstanding bravery on the battlefield.

14   the right to acquire and own land; immunity from arrest without a warrant from a court; a favourable taxation regime which meant that the pogłowne generalne or general poll tax was the only direct tax to which they were supposed to contribute; participation in the pospolite ruszenie - levée en masse - the mobilisation of armed forces as a quid pro quo for lower taxation. In due course the pospolite ruszenie was eventually replaced in large measure by professional forces; a monopoly of appointment to official administrative posts at local and national level including the local gród courts to hear criminal cases, county courts - sądy ziemskie - sitting in the county town, to hear civil suits, and the boundary courts of the podkomorzy, to judge land disputes; until 1795 the exclusive right to enter the clergy; provision to receive an education; until 1761 to try their serfs for major offences; the ability to travel without restriction anywhere in Polish and Lithuanian Commonwealth; following the first partition of Poland by Russia: privileged status of military service, including release from forced recruitment, the shortening of service from 15 to 10 years, and access to officer ranks; preference in access to secondary level schools in Poland and higher education in the Empire.

15   In 1505 the Sejm passed the Act of Nihil Novi nisi commune consensus.

16   The żupan was a long robe, usually reaching to below the knees, opened in the front, with long sleeves. Originally an outer garment, it gradually became made from lighter fabrics,

including silk.

17   A kontusz worn over a żupan was a flared over-coat in the form of long robe, usually of a vivid colour, with the lining of a contrasting hue, a set of decorative buttons down the front. The sleeves were long and loose, so in warmer weather could be untied, and thrown over the back. In winter a fur lining could be attached to the kontusz, or a delia worn over it – essentially a cloak usually fashioned from wool, cotton, or velvet, and finished with fur.

18   A pas kontuszowy was a wide sash some 40 cm wide and anything from 3 to 4.5 metres in length, and was used to tie around the kontusz. The fabric would be covered with varied designs, with the most luxurious sashes being made with silk and gold. Folded in half and wrapped around the body, the belt served as a pocket for money and documents. The more ornate sashes had up to four sides and could be folded in a number of ways so as to reveal various designs: for example, bright side for a wedding, dark side for a funeral, or colour coordinated with the kontush. The belt could also serve as a table decoration – placed at the centre along the table cloth.

19   Magnateria – magnates also known as karmazyni - crimsons, from the colour of their boots. Extremely wealthy, owning a large number of villages, estates, and serfs; Średnia szlachta or folwarczna szlachta - middle nobility, owners of one or more villages or estate, together with a small number of serfs, making up some 40% of all Polish nobility; Drobna szlachta - petty nobility, owning little or no land at all, sub-categories of which included: szlachta czastkowa: [partial nobility] part owners of estates, sharing serfs and resources with their neighbours; szlachta zagrodowa: [farming nobility] owner of a very small parcel of land with no serfs who had to work the land themselves; szlachta czynszowa: [rental nobility] tenants or leaseholders, formed a very large proportion of the petty nobility; szlachta sluzebna: [nobility of servants] nobles working on larger estates in roles such as stewards or land agents; szlachta bezrolna [landless nobility] possessing neither land nor serfs, and working as tenant farmers, labourers, soldiers and the like; szlachta brukowa [pavement nobility] small in number living in towns.

20   Herbarz Polski - Polish Armorial, Lwów, 1738.

21   The description of armorial bearings.

22   Herbarz Polski Niesieckiego, S. J. Powiększony Tom 8, 1841, pp 97

Powinna być panna rozczesana, w koronie na głowie, ręce obie do góry rozszerzone i trochę podniesione mająca, w sukni, tylko po ramiona gołe ręce, siedząca na niedźwiedziu czarnym, w lewą tarczy bieżącym, prawa noga przednia jak do biegu podniesiona u niego, w polu żółtym. W hełmie nad koroną między dwiema jelenimi rogami pół niedźwiedzia większe, obróconego w lewą tarczy, jakby siedzącego, nogę przednią spuścił, w prawej różą trzyma.

23   Or, a maiden affronté ducally crowned habited in purpura crowned or arms extended and supported on a passant bear sable, all proper. Issuant out of a ducal crown a demi-bear sable sinister supporting in dexter paw a rose gules, barbed, slipped and seeded between a pair of upright attires or, all proper.

24   Dexter and sinister are terms used in heraldry. Dexter means to the right from the viewpoint of the bearer of the shield, and likewise Sinister to the left. Insofar as the arms used by the Gan family are concerned Niesiecki is mistaken, the bear in the shield faces dexter but the half-bear in the crest, as detailed in the 1799 court deposition is in fact sinister.

25   The legend is included in Polish armorial "Orbis Polonus" assembled by Szymon Okolski in 1641–1643.

26   Sweyn was minded to keep the dowry for his own use, arranged for a bear to be put into Clotilda's bedchamber. However, through the power of prayer, and the use of her belt, the princess managed to tame the animal and next morning was able to ride out on the back of a bear, using the belt as a rein. Overcome by the sight and the obvious miracle, Sweyn asked his cousin for forgiveness and returned her dowry. In time the princess married the Prince of Lorraine, with whom she had seven sons, two of whom settled in Poland, near Rawa. In memory of their mother's

miraculous deliverance, they adopted as the family coat of arms a depiction of a virginal princess with a crown on her head, sitting on a black bear.

Notes

27 Juliusz Ostrowski, Heraldic book of Polish Families, Warsaw 1897.

28 17 March 1921 Constitution of the Republic of Poland - Article 96. All citizens are equal before the law. Public offices are accessible in equal measure to all, on conditions prescribed by the law. The Republic of Poland does not recognize privileges of birth or of estate, or any coats of arms, family or other titles, with the exception of those of learning, office, or profession. A Polish citizen may not accept foreign titles or orders without the permission of the President of the Republic.

29 *Rody Szlacheckie Imperium Rosyjskiego Pochodzące z Polski* dr Jan Ciechanowicz cz 5 *Noble Houses of the Russian Empire Originating in Poland*, part 5, dated 2 July to be found at kronikihistoryczne.blogspot.com/2019/07/rody-szlacheckie-imperium-rosyjskiego_74.html

30 Present day western Latvia

31 Present-day northern Latvia and southern Estonia

32 Zygmunt II August's raid on Livonia,1557. The Livonian War (1558–1583) was fought for control of Old Livonia (in the territory of present-day Estonia and Latvia), when the Union of the Grand Duchy of Lithuania and the Kingdom of Poland (later Commonwealth), together with other coalitions including Denmark–Norway, and the Kingdom of Sweden fought against Russia.

33 Lithuanian State Historical Archives Vilnius, zesp. 391, inv. 1, Vol. 992, pp. 15 to 20 - 1799 countersigned 1829 in Polish

34 in 1578 the King was deprived, by the Sejm - Plebeiorum Nobilitato - of his power to create new grants of ennoblement, other than for outstanding bravery on the battlefield.

35 Under King Zygmunt III, Polish–Lithuanian Commonwealth was involved in a number of wars and battles in the period 1617 and 1620, including: the Polish–Swedish War, 1617–18; The Battle of Orynin,1618 against Crimean Tatars; and the Battle of Humenné, 1619, involving the King's elite mercenary unit, the Lisowczycy; and the Polish-Ottoman War, 1620–21.

36 The patronymic has been used whenever possible to help

distinguish between individuals from different generations given the propensity of the Gan family to use a limited number of Christian names, such as Tomasz.

37   Uruski Seweryn, *Rodzina Herbarz Szlachty Polskiej T4*, Kosiński Adam Amilkar; Włodarski Aleksander, Warszawa, 1907, pp61 - 62

38   *Op. Cit. Rody Szlacheckie Imperium Rosyjskiego Pochodzące z Polski*

39   Lithuanian State Historical Archives Vilnius, p. 391, z. 4, No. 1035, p.3; https://pl.wikipedia.org/wiki/Ejgirdy [accessed 10 March 2020].
Op. Cit. Lithuanian State Historical Archives Vilnius, zesp. 391, inv. 1, Vol. 992, pp15 - 20 - 1799 countersigned 1829 in Polish.

41   Uruski Seweryn, *Rodzina Herbarz Szlachty Polskiej T4*, Kosiński Adam Amilkar; Włodarski Aleksander, Warszawa, 1907, pp 90 – 91 The early Heraldic/Nobility Courts list the family name variously as Hahn, Han, von Han, Hahnów, Gan, and Ganów. There is also reference to the three branches of the family, one that retained the correct name Gan, the second that changed it to Gano, and the third that became Ganolipski.

42   Lithuanian State Historical Archives Vilnius, zesp. 391, inv. 1, Vol. 992, pp15-20 – 1799.

43   Czesław Malewski*, Rodziny szlacheckie na Litwie w XIX wieku Powiaty lidzki, oszmiański i wileński*, Warszawa, 2016

44   Today known as Ashmyany, Halshany, Trabi, and Juraciški respectively.

45   Elektorów Poczet którzy niegdyś głosowali na elektóv Jana Kazimierza roku 1648, Jana III. roku 1674, Augusta II. roku 1697, i Stanisława Augusta roku 1764, p86

46   Herbarz Polski, Kaspra Niesieckiego, 1839, p68

47   LVIA, Zesp. 604, inv. 44, vol. 71, s. 208v, nr. 24

48   Dziesięcina [a tithe] equivalent of 1.09 hectares

49   Kevin Schürer, Local Population Studies Society Conference, *'Paths to Marriage; Courtship in England and Wales, c1700-*

c1945', Oxford, October 2019

50 https://www.osada.org/dubicki/dubicki2-pl.php [accessed 10 March 2020]

51 The names Dzieniesienko, Gajduczenko appear in the list for both villages, so could be the same person or they may be related

52 Czesław Malewski, *Rodziny szlacheckie na Litwie w XIX wieku Powiaty lidzki, oszmiański i wileński,* Warszawa, 2016, p263

53 Jerzy Lukowski, The peasantry of Poland-Lithuania on the eve of the French revolution, *History of European Ideas*, 1990 vol. 12 No. 3, pp377

54 Jean-Jacques Rousseau, *Considerations on the Government of Poland and on its Proposed Reformation,* April 1772 (completed but not published) p12, [accessed 2 August 2020] https://www.files.ethz.ch/isn/125482/5016_Rousseau_Consid erations_on_the_Government_of_Poland.pdf

55 Jalonen, Jussi, "On Behalf of the Emperor: The Finnish Guard's Campaign to Poland, 1831." *The Slavonic and East European Review*, vol. 88, no. 3, 2010, pp468–494. *JSTOR*, www.jstor.org/stable/20780432 [Accessed 5 May 2020].

56 Joseph Straszewicz, Pierre Simon Ballanche, *Emilie Plater: sa vie et sa mort,* 1835, pp331-332; Joachim Lelewel, Histoire de Pologne: L'histoire de la Pologne racontée par un oncle à ses neveux. La Pologne renaissante, Librairie polonaise, 1844, p321

57 Henryk Moscicki, Powstanie 1831 Roku Na Litwie –

Wspomnienia Uczestników, Wilno, 1931 p104

58 F. Wrotnowski, *Zbiór pamiętników o powstaniu Litwy w 1831 roku, Leipzig,* 1875, p242

59 Tomasz Gan c1754-1831, by a process of elimination, the son of Kazimierz and great-grandson of Piotr

60 The University did not reopen until 1919, following Polish independence.

61 Adam Zamoyski, *Poland A History, 2009,* Harper Press, ISBN: 978-0-00-728275-3, p235

62 *Pan Tadeusz, czyli ostatni zajazd na Litwie. Historia szlachecka z roku 1811 i 1812 we dwunastu księgach wierszem, Paris, 1834*

63 Czesław Miłosz, *The History of Polish literature*, IV, Romanticism, p. 228. Google Books. University of California Press, 1983. ISBN 0-520-04477-0

64 "Pan Tadeusz Poem: Five things you need to know about this epic Polish masterpiece". https://www.independent.co.uk/news/world/pan-tadeusz-poem-adam-mickiewicz-epic-polish-poland-google-doodle-a8978516.html, [accessed 10 May 2020]

65 Adam Mickiewicz, *Pan Tadeusz: The Last Foray in Lithuania*, Translated from Polish by Bill Johnston, 2018, Archipelago Books, ISBN: 978-1-939810-01-4

66 Ludwik Mierosławski (1814-1878) General, writer, poet, historian and political activist. Having taken part in the November 1831 Uprising, emigrated to France after its failure where he became active involved in various Polish emigre organizations, particularly the Polish Democratic Society (*Towarzystwo Demokratyczne Polskie or TDP*), joining its executive in 1845 and in 1846 was appointed by the Society as Commander for the Greater Poland Uprising of 1846. Betrayed by a fellow conspirator he was arrested in February 1846 by the Prussian authorities, and sentenced to death, but saved by a general amnesty in March1848. Returned to Poland to lead insurgents in battles against Prussia later the same year, but surrendered in May 1848; arrested again, but released in the July. Later in 1848 and 1849 he fought for the insurgents in Baden and the Palatinate, and then returned to France. Took part in the 1863 January Uprising, as the first of four dictators of the Uprising, but fell out with the National Government, and refused to resign. After returning to France, he no longer played a significant role in the political life of emigrants, and died in Paris in oblivion and poverty. "Despite everything, he became a symbol of Polish and European revolutionary struggles and one of the leading figures of the nineteenth-century democratic left. He went down in history despite the scale of his defeats." Prof. Andrzej Szwarc. [accessed 10 May 2020]. https://www.polskieradio.pl/39/156/Artykul/1547032, Ludwik-Mieroslawski-%E2%80%93-general-kleska

Notes

67   Remembrance of the Dalewski
http://www.wilnoteka.lt/artykul/wspomnienie-o-dalewskich
[accessed 11 May 2020]

68   Encyclopaedia of 1848 Revolutions
https://www.ohio.edu/chastain/ip/lithua.htm, Accessed 11 May 2020. The Encyclopaedia is fascinating in that it provides some 350 separate entries relating to revolutions world-wide that took place during the course of 1848

69   Franciszek Dalewski (1825-1904) Social activist, and conspirator. Studied at the Gymnasium in Wilno, expelled in 1846, for unacceptable behaviour, losing his right to attend university. Formed the *Zwiazek Bratni Mlodziezy Litewskiej* - Union of the Brotherhood of Lithuanian Youth - with his brother Alexander, in 1846. Initially sentenced to death, commuted to 15 years hard labour in 1850 at Nerczyńsk, Siberia, returned to Wilno in 1859 under an amnesty. Took part in the January 1863 Uprising member of the Provincial Committee of Lithuania, Provincial Provisional Government. Sentenced to 12 years of hard labour, sentence increased to 20 years due to recidivism. Released in 1883, following an amnesty, settled in Warsaw, where he worked on the Dąbrowa railway.

70   Aleksander Dalewski (1827-1862) Patriot, political activist, and conspirator. Studied at the Wilno Poviat school, and later at the Gymnasium (1844–1846), but did not graduate. Worked as a teacher. Sentenced to 10 years hard labour in 1850 at Nerczyńsk, Siberia, returned under an amnesty to Wilno in 1859, and was buried at the Rossa Cemetery.

71   Florjan Danowski (1822-1903) Exiled in 1850 for 8 years hard labour, Nerczyńsk, Siberia; returned in 1858. In 1863 exiled to Tomsk, Siberia; returned in 1878 and settled in Karolinów, central Poland where he lived until his death.

72   Edward Żeligowski (1816-1864) aka Antoni Sowa, poet, translator (especially of Russian literature), publicist. Author of the dramatic fantasy "Jordan" and others. 1833-1836 he studied at the University of Dorpat in Estonia, interned for participating in a secret patriotic association. 1842, he settled in Vilnius, where he became involved in the Brotherhood of Lithuanian Youth. Deported to Siberia in 1851, eventually settled in France and later in Switzerland.

73   Jakób Wilhelm Kasper Gieysztor (1827-1897) Polish Patriot,
      diarist, and antiquarian bookseller. He graduated in 1844 with
      a silver medal at the Instytut Szlachecki in Wilno, and went on
      to study at the Law Faculty of the St. Petersburg University. In
      1848, on the eve of final exams, he returned to Wilno to try to
      prevent the uprising being orchestrated by the Dalewski
      brothers. After which he settled in the Ignacogród estate, where
      he took up farming. He founded a reading room, and a school
      that taught, without any sense of irony in Lithuanian. In 1858,
      in the formulation of his ideas on peasant reform, he wrote his
      first publication: *Głos szlachcica do swych współbraci o wolności
      i równości kmiecej - A nobleman's voice to his brothers about
      freedom and equality.* A vociferous advocate for the abolition of
      serfdom, he was the first to grant freedom to the serfs in
      Kiejdanach, and whilst his campaign had some success locally
      he was unable to persuade his peers in the rest of Lithuania to
      do likewise, before the Russians inevitably did so in 1861. At
      the outset of the January 1863 Uprising he became President of
      the Department of Provincial Administration of the Provisional
      Government of Lithuania, and as such was arrested in July
      1863. In 1865, he was initially sentenced to 12 years hard labour
      at Usol, in Siberia. In 1868 he was transferred to Irkutsk, to
      complete his period in exile, where he was permitted to trade in
      footwear. In 1872 he was allowed to return to Poland. Initially he
      settled in Suwałki, and finally in Warsaw. In 1882 he opened an
      antiquarian bookshop, the contents of which were in due course
      donated to the Branicki library at Sucha. Gieysztor was the
      author of extensive memoirs that are a valuable source of
      historical information for the years 1857-1865.

74   Gieysztor, Jakób, i Tadeusz Korzon, Pamiętniki Jakóba
      Gieysztora z Lat 1857-1865. Wilno: Bibljoteka Pamiętników,
      1913, pp22-24. The memoirs were written in six parts, but only
      that relating to the years 1857-1865 were published. However,
      the events of 1848 and 1849 were thought to be of such
      significance that they were included in the Introduction.

75   Gieysztor's family estate at Kiejdanach some 66 miles (107 km)
      north of Wilno.

76   It is unlikely that Mierosławski visited Wilno at this time, given
      that he was fighting in Baden and the Palatinate, see footnote

64, but the use of his name and reputation would nevertheless have been quite persuasive

77   Stefan Gieysztor's family estate at Zabieliszek some 102 miles (164 km) south of Kiejdanach, shown on the map detailing estates, villages, and land held by members of the Gan Family from 1620 to 1939.

78   Zabieliszek to Wilno is a distance of some 45 miles (73 km).

79   http://maps.mapywig.org/m/WIG_maps/series/025K/P35-S40-E_RUDA_JAWORSKA_1930.jpg [accessed 25 June 2020]

80   [Accessed 25 June 2020]
http://maps.mapywig.org/m/German_maps/series/100K_Kd WR/400dpi/KdwR_Q28_Wenzowiec_1914_400dpi.jpg

81   A large farmhouse with its various farm buildings.

82   Morg (Plural: Morgi) was a unit of land measurement used in pre-war Poland equivalent to approximately 0.6 hectares. Similar in nomenclature the morgen was used in Germany, the Netherlands, and the Dutch colonies, including South Africa and Taiwan. The size of a morgen varies from ½ to 2½ acres, which approximates from 0.2 to 1 hectare.

83   The marka was the unit of currency in Poland between 1917 and 1924. 100 fenigów was equivalent to 1 marka. Until 1917 four currencies circulated in Poland – the Russian ruble, the German Papiermark, the German Ostruble, and the Austro-Hungarian krone. On December 9, 1916 the Polish Loan Bank (*Polska Krajowa Kasa Pożyczkowa*) was established and the Polish marka (plural: marek, marki) was introduced, equivalent in value to the German mark. The Reichsbank guaranteed the stability of the new currency up to 1 billion mark. As part of the financial reform of 1924 the Bank Polski was designated as the new central bank of Poland and the marka was exchanged for a new gold-based currency, the zloty. The exchange rate was set at 1.8 million marek to 1 złoty. In 1922, half a million marks amounted to some $84. By 1924 half a million marks was worth less than 1 złoty, in fact about 30 groszy, or about £12 in today's money. The money Ludwika received in 1927 represented a good return, not least because it represented something like half the annual wage of a farm labourer at the time.

84   Franciszek was not named or involved as he was at that time already living in Buczacz, some 400 miles (640 km) away in south-east Poland.

85   Of the nineteen people present, 14 signed the agreement, and 5 who were illiterate asked for the document to be signed on their behalf.

86   1 Tithe =1.08 hectares. 1 hectare = 2.47 acres.

87   About £16,500 in today's money.

88   A Pood (plural: pudy) = 40 funt - Polish pound. Used in Lithuania, Russia, Belarus, and Ukraine. In 1899 it was set approximately at 16.38 kilograms (36.11 pounds). Pood was first mentioned in the 12th century, unlike funt, which came into use in the 14th century. Together with other weight measurements used in Imperial Russia, the USSR officially abolished the pood in 1924. But the term remained in widespread use, as demonstrated here, to at least until the 1940s.

89   The contract was for 12 Pudy i.e. 12 x 16.38 kilos/litres = 196.6 kilos/litres or 1.96 hectolitres. At the time the price of rye was 5.54 grms per 1 hectolitre (100 litres), and the price of gold, was £4.25 per ounce (28 grms). £4.25 in 1930 is the equivalent of £250 in today's money. Hence the value of the contract was approximately £100 per year.

90   The offence is not specified but likely to have been that he was a land-owner.

91   Folwark Han was situated near the village of Ruda Jaworska, in the Powiat (District /County) of Słonim, in the Województwo (Province) of Nowogródek.

Whilst the village was in the Powiat of Słonim the family estate was literally just over the county boundary in the Powiat of Nowogródek. This helps explain why family documents were validated at either Słonim [Slonim], the county town of the Powiat of Słonim some 10 miles south-east of Folwark Han, or at Zdzięcioł [Dzyatlava], some 15 miles to the north-east, it being the county town of the Powiat of Nowogródek, not to be confused with the city of Nowogródek [Navahrudak] the Capital of the whole województwo which was some 37 miles to the north-east

Folwark Han, and the smallest of all of Poland's wojewódzkich capital cities, with a population of almost 10,000.

In 1928 the population of Ruda Jaworska was 686. The railway was 22 miles away in Skrzbowce, the nearest post office and telephone were in Kozlowszczyzna, fifteen miles distant, and the telegraph was 23 miles away in Nowojelnia.

Słonim's population was 9,643, with its own Justice of the Peace, four Catholic churches, one Orthodox, one mosque, and two synagogues. It also had one state and one private high school. Local industry included: grain mills, sawmills, brickworks, a tannery, a machine factory, and a brandy factory.

The population of Zdzięcioł was 3,008, with its own Justice of the Peace, one Catholic church, one Orthodox, four synagogues, a municipal hospital, ambulance, electricity factory, slaughterhouse, veterinary clinic, together with various mills and tanneries. The railway was 7 miles away in Nowojelnia.

The Województwo of Nowogródek, which was composed of seven powiats, with eight cities and 89 towns, suffered much neglect

whilst under Russian control and when Poland gained independence in 1918 it was one of the poorest in Poland. In 1921 the literacy rate was only 45%, with only a moderate improvement to 65% by 1931. The road and rail networks were almost non-existent. There was less than 450 miles of railway in the Województwo, and Nowogródek was not even on the main

line and reachable only by narrow-gauge track. As at 1 January 1928, there were only 123 cars and eight motorcycles registered in the whole of the Województwo.

Agriculture was by far the most important source of livelihood, arable crops produced for milling in the 611 flour mills including rye (65%), barley (13%), wheat (7%), with potatoes being the other major crop, whilst livestock comprised cattle 37%, pigs 22%, sheep 21%, and horses 20%. The abundance of forest meant that wood processing and wood-based manufacture were important in the region, employing some 36% of working population. The production of flax steadily increased in the period up to 1939 with the consequent development of spinning mills and linen weaving. Other industrial enterprises in the

Województwo included: mills, saw mills, milk processing plants, tar and turpentine factories, brickyards, soft drinks factories, tanneries and a small number of distilleries. The most important commercial centres were Nowogródek, Baranowicze, Lida, and Słonim.

The ethnic breakdown of the population of 800,761 may be summarised as 53% Polish, 37% Belarus, 7% Jewish, and 3% other nationalities, which almost mirrors the results of the 1931 census which gave the percentage breakdown of mother tongue as 53% Polish, 39% Belarus, 7% Yiddish, 1% as Russian, with the balance made up of Ukrainian, German, and Czech. Insofar as religious affiliation was concerned 51% described themselves as Orthodox, 39% as Catholic, 7.0% Jewish, and 3% other. The figures should only be taken as a rough approximation,

something Stalin certainly did managing to convince the Tehran Conference of 1943, that area was predominantly Belarussian and as such must be handed over to the Soviet, with the Polish population being forcibly resettled.

Sources for the above note include: the 1928 Polish Business Directory *"Księga Adresowa Polski (Wraz z w.m. Gdańskiem) dla Han dlu, Przemyslu, Rzemiosl i Rolnictwa"* indexed by Ellen Sadove Renck.
https://jri-poland.org/bizdir/start.htm
https://www.jewishgen.org/databases/Poland/NowogrodskieTowns.htm

https://en.wikipedia.org/wiki/Nowogródek_Voivodeship_(1919–1939) [accessed 5 August 2020]

92   There is a reference to that effect in the document completed on his arrest by the NKVD on 9 December 1939.

93   The aiguillettes and cords that Franciszek is wearing are unusual, normally worn over the right shoulder, these worn on the left were awarded to soldiers after their initial training as an indication that following independence the newly formed Polish army was ready for action.

94   The 5th Kaniow *Ułan (Light Cavalry)* Regiment (5 Pułk Ułanów Kaniowskich, 6 puł) was formed in 1917, as part of Polish II Corps in Russia, disbanded after the battle of Kaniow in May

1918. Formed again in December 1918, as a merger of 6th Ułan Regiment of Lwów and 6th Ułan regiment from Odessa, and disbanded again in 1919. The Ułan were Polish-Lithuanian light cavalry armed with lances, sabres and pistols. The 6th Field Artillery Regiment (Szósty Pułk Artylerii Polowej) part of the Sixth Infantry Division, and fought in both the Polish–Ukrainian War, and Polish–Soviet War. In January 1921, the regiment was stationed near Ożydów, some forty miles east of Lwow, where it remained as part of the 6th Army reserves. In May 1921, the regiment was moved to Stanisławów, when during the refurbishment of the barracks, the regiment's units were stationed in the surrounding villages.

95 Franciszek Gan is wearing the uniform of a Senior Constable to which rank he was promoted in 1934.

96 History of Buczacz during World War II quoted from Norman Davies (1996), Europe: A History, pp 1034-1035, Oxford University Press.

97 My father, Ludwik, had a clear affinity with my maternal grandmother's Turczanski branch of the family, some of whom remained in Poland after the Second World War, whilst others formed part of the Polish diaspora in England. A collection of letters, found after my father's death, seem to indicate that my father, continued to maintain contact with his maternal cousins in Poland as best he could. These included Janina Turczanska who married Zdzisław Kosecki and lived on Marszałkowska in Warsaw with their daughter Teresa, whom I was able to visit in the early 1970's. My cousin Edward Zielinski and great-uncle Julian perished in Auschwitz in 1941 and 1942 respectively. Julian's grandson Zdzisław Denkowski, remained in contact, most latterly with my mother, until his untimely death in 2019. Insofar as other relatives, who also took the difficult decision to live in exile rather than return to communist Poland, I recall the great kindness shown to me and my brother in the 1960s, by Józef and Maria Turczanski, the parents of Henryk and Basia, whom we visited regularly when they were living near us in Melton Mowbray. Henryk spent most of his adult life in south-east London, with a brief sojourn in the USA, whilst his sister Basia still lives Birmingham. Although they are my second cousins (twice removed), they remain an integral part of the extended Gan family.

The extracts from the Turczanski family tree detailed in Appendix 3 graphically illustrate the relationship between the two branches of the family.

98 Op. Cit. Norman Davies

99 Polish State Police Order No. 381, Tarnopol, 29 August, 1938.

100 Polish State Police Order No. 404, Tarnopol, 1 June, 1939.

101 Also known as the Polish-Bolshevik War - Wojna Bolszewicka

102 Known as Lemberg during the Austro-Hungarian occupation and currently as Lviv.

103 Canadian Institute of Ukrainian Studies
http://www.encyclopediaofukraine.com/picturedisplay.asp?lin
kpath=pic\L\V\Lviv_population%20table.jpg
[accessed 25 May 2020]

104 Snyder Timothy, *The Reconstruction of Nations : Poland, Ukraine, Lithuania, Belarus 1569-1999*, Yale University Press, New Haven, 2003, 0-300-10586-x, p123

105 Ibid p328

106 Bartov Omer, *Anatomy of a Genocide: The Life and Death of aTown Called Buczacz*, Simon & Schuster, New York 2018, 978-1-4516-8453 7.

107 Ibid. pp130-133

108 Op. Cit. Snyder pp156-159

109 "Decision to commence investigation into Katyń Massacre", Kuźniar-Plota, Małgorzata, Prosecutor - Commission for the Prosecution of Crimes against the Polish Nation; Instytut Pamięci Narodowej (Institute of National Remembrance) https://ipn.gov.pl/en/news/77,Decision-to-commence-investigation-into-Katyn-Massacre.html [accessed 29 May 2020]

On 30 November 2004, the Commission for the Prosecution of Crimes against the Polish Nation in Warsaw issued a decision to commence investigations, case no. S 38/04/Zk, into the "mass murder, by shooting, of not less than 21,768 Polish citizens, for the purpose of liquidating a part of the Polish national group, during the period between 5 March and an unspecified date in

Notes

1940 in Moscow, Kharkov, Smolensk, Katyń , Kalinin (now Tver), and other locations on the territory of the Union of Soviet Socialist Republics by its state functionaries acting on instructions from the authorities of their state, which was then allied with the Third Reich, the victims being: soldiers of the Polish Army and Border Defence Corps, officers of the State Police and of other Polish state services - prisoners of war taken by the Red Army and accommodated in "special prison camps" of the NKVD in Kozelsk, Starobelsk and Ostashkov, civilians arrested for being, among other things „(...) intelligence agents and gendarmes, spies and saboteurs, former landowners, factory owners and officials (...)"

and placed in prisons on the Eastern Territories of the Republic of Poland occupied by the USSR, as a result of the implementation of the criminal resolution by the Politburo of the Central Committee of the All-Union Communist Party (Bolsheviks) reached in Moscow on 5 March 1940...

110 Fischer, Benjamin B., "The Katyń Controversy: Stalin's Killing Field". *Studies in Intelligence*, (1999–2000 - Winter). https://www.cia.gov/library/center-for-the-study-of-intelligence/csi-publications/csi-studies/studies/winter99-00/art6.html#rft7 [accessed 29 May 2010]

111 Op.Cit. Kuźniar-Plota, Małgorzata

112 Cienciala, Anna M., Materski, Wojciech, *Katyń : A Crime without Punishment*, 2007, Yale University Press, 978-0-300-10851-4, p30.

113 Zawodny, Janusz K. *Death in the Forest: The Story of the Katyń Forest Massacre*, University of Notre Dame Press, 1962, 978-0-268-00849-9, p77.

114 Op.Cit. Fischer, Benjamin B.

115 Op.Cit. Kuźniar-Plota, Małgorzata.

116 Weinberg, Gerhard, *A World at Arms*, Cambridge University Press, 2005, 978-0-521-61826-7, p107.

117 Politburo of the All-Union Communist Party (Bolsheviks)

     Central Committee ACP (b)

118 Wasilewski, Witold, "Evidence for the March 5th 1940 Decision of the Political Bureau of the Central Committee of All-Union

Communist Party (Bolsheviks) to Mass Murder Polish Citizens" *Katyń : State -Sponsored Extermination: Collection of Essays,* Ed. Szornert, Xlibris, 2012, 978-1477155790, p43

[119] Kalinin is 125 miles north west of Moscow.

[120] Medonye, in Polish Miednoje.

[121] Op.Cit. Kużniar-Plota, Małgorzata.

[122] Polish translation of the original Soviet document:

NKWD Nr 012/2 kwietnia 1940 r. m. Moskwa Ściśle tajne Do rąk wlasnych

Komendant obozu jenieckiego w Ostaszkowie Major tow. Borysowice

Po otrzymaniu tej lity beszwłocznie' wysjele do m. Kallina do dyspozycji naczelnika Zarządu. NKWD obwodu kallnińskiego niżej wymienionych jeńcow wojennych orzetrzymywanych w obozie ostaszkowskim: Naczelnik Zarządu NKWD ZSRR dz jencow wojwnnych kapitan bezpleczeńatwa państwowego (Soprunienka) Jeńcow skierowano na śmierć między 5.04. a 07.04.1940 r.

KVD No. 012/2 - April 1940 - Moscow City

Highly Secret For your own hands

to the Komendant POW camp in Ostaszków Major Borysowice

After receiving this list, you will send without delay to Kalinin for the disposal of the head of the NKVD Board of the Kaliningrad District the following prisoners of war detained in the Ostashkov camp: [there follows a list of 99 people – including]

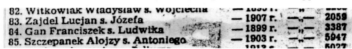

Signed (Soprunienka)

Head of the NKVD USSR State Security Board of Prisoners of War

Prisoners were sent to death between 5.04. and 07.04.1940

[123] [Accessed 30 May 2020]
www.policjapanstwowa.pl/Ksiega_Cmentarna_Miednoje_Tom1.

pdf p199
http://policjapanstwowa.pl/index-189.htm

125 Op.Cit. Kuźniar-Plota, Małgorzata.

126 Wasilewska Irena, *Suffer Little Children,* Maxlove Publishing, London 1946 p11.

127 Czesiek was always known by his family nickname of Czes.

128 Piesakowski, Tomasz, *The Fate of Poles in the USSR 1939–1989,* Gryf, 1990, p77, 0-901342-24-6.

129 Anders, W, *An Army in Exile: The Story of the Second Polish Corps,* (Allied Forces Series), 1949, re-printed 1981, The Battery Press Inc, Nashville, 978-0898390438 quoted in https://artsandculture.google.com/exhibit/general-władysław-anders-difficult-choices-polish-history-museum/LgJyA445wKN0JA?hl=en [accessed 6 June 2020]

130 The original death certificate issued by the Soviet authorities is in the family archive.

131 In 1935 the Iranian government requested that all countries with

which it had diplomatic relations call the country by its Persian name, Iran.

132 Ironic given that the family name was originally the German Von Hahn.

133 Op. Cit. Wasilewska Irena, pp108-109.

134 Air Chief Marshall Sir Michael Armitage, "The Polish Apprentices at Halton", *Journal No. 36, 2006, Royal Air Force Historical Society,* pp43-51.

135 https://artsandculture.google.com/exhibit/passage-to-india-polish -history-museum/FQKCQq9LDKemIg?hl=en [accessed 9 June 2020]

136 Op. Cit. Anders, W.

137 https://www.polishexilesofww2.org/archival-lists-polish-2nd-corps, [accessed 10 June 2020].

138 The Historian of the U.S. Department of State is responsible, under law, for the preparation and publication of the *Foreign Relations of the United States* (*FRUS*) series that presents the official documentary historical record of major U.S. foreign policy decisions.

139 https://commons.wikimedia.org/w/index.php?curid=7823226 [accessed 12 June] 2020 Mosedschurte, June 1, 2009, GFDL.

140 At the time the two conflicting Polish Governments were colloquially referred to as the 'Lublin Poles', where the Polish Provisional Government was formed and unsurprisingly the Polish Government in Exile as the 'London Poles'.

141 [Accessed 20 June 2020], Radek. S, January 2007, GFDL https://upload.wikimedia.org/wikipedia/commons/8/8d/Curz on_line_en.svg

142 Foreign Relations of the United States: Diplomatic Papers, The Conference of Berlin (The Potsdam Conference), 1945, Vol. II, https://history.state.gov/historicaldocuments/frus1945Berlinv 02/pg_1152 [accessed 13 June 2020]

143 Ibid. p1148

144 Ibid. p1153

145 Ibid. p1153

146 Ibid. p1152

147 The final delimitation of the western frontier of Poland take places 45 years later, at the Treaty on the Final Settlement with Respect to Germany in 1990.

148 Op. Cit. Foreign Relations of the United States: Diplomatic Papers pp1490-1492.

149 Ibid. p1495

150 Davies, Norman, *The Anders Army, An Odyssey Across Three Continents*, 2015, Osprey, pp530-531, ISBN 9781472816030

151 Hansard, 5 June 1946, https://api.parliament.uk/historic-hansard/commons/1946/jun/05/foreign-affairs#column_2117 [accessed 14 June 2020].

152 Mark Ostrowski, *"To Return to Poland or Not to Return" – The dilemma Facing the Polish Armed Forces at the end of the Second World War*, Unpublished PhD Thesis, University of London, School of Slavonic and East European Studies, 1996, p12.

153 Ibid. pp381-383

154 Hansard 20 March 1946 vol. 420 cc1882 https://api.parliament.uk/historic-hansard/commons/1946/mar/20/polish-armed-forces-government-policy [accessed 15 June 2020].

155 Hansard, 22 May 1946 vol. 423 cc301-302, https://api.parliament.uk/historic-hansard/commons/1946/may/22/polish-armed-forces-repatriation-and [accessed 16 June 2020].

156 Polish Resettlement Bill, Hansard 31 January 1947 vol. 432 c1273 [accessed 16 June 2020] https://api.parliament.uk/historic-hansard/commons/1947/jan/31/polish-resettlement-bill#column_1273

157 Hansard 25 March 1948 vol. 448 cc343W https://api.parliament.uk/historic-hansard/written-answers/1948/mar/25/poles-naturalisation#column_343w [accessed 16 June 2020].

158 Blaszczyk, Agata, *The Resettlement of Polish refugees after the Second World War,* [accessed 16 June 2020] https://www.fmreview.org/resettlement/blaszczyk

159 Holmes, Colin, *John Bull's Island: Immigration and British Society, 1871-1971*, Macmillan, 1988 p212 https://books.google.co.uk/books?id=cdq9CgAAQBAJ&q=168#v=snippet&q=polish&f=false [accessed 16 June 2020].

160 A Class W(T) Reservist was a part-time volunteer in the Territorial Force of the British Army. As such he did not receive any pay, nor required to wear uniform, but could be re-called if required. It was specifically designed 'for all those soldiers whose services are deemed to be more valuable to the country in civil rather than military employment'.

161 Obóz, means Camp in English.

162 Riddlesworth Hall became a prep-school in 1946. Its most famous alumna was Diana, Princess of Wales.

163 A backwash minder passes wool slivers through a back-washing machine, which reconditions them by the addition of oil, cleanses them, and improves their colour.

164 A Wool Comber is any person employed in the wool combing industry. It is the process by which wool is carded to lay the tangled fibres into roughly parallel strands and then disentangled and straightened so that they can be more easily drawn out for spinning. A combing machine separates the noils (short, knobbly fibres for textured yarns) from the tops (long, smooth fibres for classic, simple yarn).

165 Ludwik took his responsibilities as paterfamilias very seriously, some might even say that on occasion to the point of being a little too intense, but given the circumstances of what they had all been through, that was to be expected. On arrival in England the whole family lived together in Bradford, but before the move to Nottingham places were found at boarding schools for both Roman and Teresa, paid for by the Committee for the Education Poles in Great Britain, which had taken on that role from the Polish Government in Exile, and was publicly funded as part of the Polish Resettlement Act of 1947.

Roman was found a place at the Frederic Chopin Secondary at Diddington Park, not far from St Neots in Huntingdonshire. Teresa meanwhile was sent to a Catholic Boarding School at Pitsford Hall, in Northamptonshire run by Polish nuns from the Sisters of the Holy Family of Nazareth, but she always spent her holidays living with Ludwik and Czesia. After Pitsford which only took pupils up to the age of sixteen, Teresa moved school with a sixth-form run by the same group of nuns at Enfield. After which, rather than go straight on to college, she took a commercial Pitman short-hand and typing course, which stood her in good stead in getting paid work during vacations, whilst studying to be a secondary-school teacher at Crewe Teacher Training College. Having gained her teaching certificate, Teresa taught in schools in Nottingham, a particularly enjoyable period in Manchester, and finally in Gloucester. Although not great in stature, Teresa commanded the greatest respect from even the largest and roughest of youths who, whilst towering over her, would carry out her every direction, knowing full well that she would brook no nonsense.

Czesiek whilst in Lebanon had studied in the Sekcja Mechaniczna in the Junacka Szkoła Kadetów (Young Soldiers Cadet School). On arrival in England in April 1947 he enrolled in the Polish Settlement Corps, from which he was discharged in

July 1949 to take a job in Bradford. He also studied part-time in the evenings for a City and Guilds Course in Machine Shop Engineering, which he successfully completed in July 1950. The following year both Roman, on leaving Diddington Park, and Czesiek were enrolled onto and successfully completed a one-year course at the Polish Agricultural College in Glasgow. For what purpose is not entirely clear, as neither had any interest in the subject. I suspect that one of the reasons may have been Ludwik's, not unreasonable predilection for the need to have some form of academic qualification, not least being in a new country and having missed out on so many years of education. It would be true to say that unlike Ludwik, neither Czesiek or Roman were academically inclined – engineering was their forte, and unlike Ludwik both were very practical. It was no surprise that they also went in to the textile trade based in Nottingham, Czesiek becoming a well-respected engineer responsible for the installation of lace-making-machinery around the world. Roman who spent all of his working life in Nottingham, after taking on a range of different jobs, including for a time that of a bus conductor, became a very much valued engineer responsible for the maintenance of lace-making-machines for one of the largest lace manufacturers in Nottingham.Prior to their respective marriages, and until such a time as Czesiek and Roman were able to buy a house to share together in Nottingham, Czesiek in between his many journeys overseas, would lodge with Ludwik and Czesia, whereas right from the start Roman was able to find his own bed-sit accommodation. There was, however, always a bed available for Czesiek, Roman, and Teresa with Ludwik and Czesia. This is one reason why it never occurred to me to call them uncle or aunty, as they have always been more akin to an elder brother or sister.

Both Czesiek and Roman were taken from us far too early, but I recall with much pleasure, many small remembrances, such as

Czesiek, when he was living with us returning to Ripley after having been paid, on a Friday evening, with a bagful of sweets; Roman who took me to my first football match – Nottingham. Forest v Aston Villa in September 1962 – Forest won 3-1; and who was responsible for helping me set up my first electric train set, with engines, rails, and other numerous essential items, bought from the various second-hand shops that were then prevalent on Arkwright Street in Nottingham; and Teresa who in 1967 managed to engineer taking me on my first visit overseas - a school trip (her school – not mine) to Belgium, where their boys were playing in a football tournament – and who no doubt out of deference to her took me under their wing, to ensure that no harm came to me, even though I was a Nottingham Forest supporter whilst they were all committed to Manchester City.

[166] This seems to be something of a family habit, Czesia and Józef's father originally had the surname Gorzynik but changed it to Gorzelnik – meaning 'Distiller', sometime before 1939, for reasons that are far from clear.

[167] Woolcomber is listed as the occupation of the father on the birth certificate of Ryszard Gan.

[168] Winston Churchill presented his *Sinews of Peace*, (the *Iron Curtain Speech*), at Westminster College in Fulton, Missouri on March 5, 1946. [accessed 13 June 2020] http://www.historyguide.org/europe/churchill.html

[169] Peter D. Stachura, Editor *The Poles in Britain 1940–2000*, Frank Cass, 2004, 0-7146-8444-9 p45.

[170] Keegan, J, *Six Armies in Normandy: From D-Day to the Liberation of Paris*, Random House, 2004, 9781844137398, p269

[171] Registered as Ryszard on his Birth Certificate.

[172] Richard's brother Michael joined him at the Becket School in 1964. Michael then went on to study at the University of Leeds and on graduating remained in the Leeds area. Until his retirement Michael spent his career working within the National Health Service in a variety of senior managerial roles in Leeds and South Yorkshire. Michael also served as a School Governor for a number of years at a leading Catholic secondary school in Leeds.

173   Notwithstanding the fact that he had attended three Roman Catholic schools, or perhaps because of it, Richard initially lapsed, having found that the Roman Catholicism remained resolutely dogmatic, refusing to accept the reality of human frailty, and not in any way adapting or adopting a more pragmatic approach to the fact that civilisation had moved on since the foundation of the Church. Ultimately made a positive decision and was received into the Church of England on 27 March 1988.

174   Chelsea College was amalgamated into King's College in 1985.

175   The University of London Institute of Education merged with University College in 2014.

176   Freemasonry, may not be a secret organisation but it is a fairly complex one. All Freemasons initially join what is colloquially known as the 'Craft', and it is the one that most non-members would be most familiar. In England the headquarters are based in Freemasons' Hall in London, and its Grand Master is currently HRH the Duke of Kent. However, there are many different subdivisions within Freemasonry including what are known as the Progressive Orders, that include the 'Mark', which are administered from Mark Masons Hall in St. James's London. The Grand Master of the Mark is at present HRH Prince Michael of Kent, the brother of The Duke of Kent. Anybody interested in finding out more about the subject could do worse than buying a copy of Richard Gan's, *Secret Handshakes and Rolled-Up Trouser Legs: The Secrets of Freemasonry - Separating Fact and Fiction,* (London, 2014), ISBN 9780853184416, pp128

177   The Military and Hospitaller Order of Saint Lazarus is one of the oldest European orders of chivalry. From its foundation the Order has been dedicated to two ideals: aid to those suffering from leprosy, and the defence of the Christian faith. Today the Order is an international ecumenical charitable organisation, whose membership is open to all men and women of the Christian faith in good standing with their own particular religious denomination.

178   The varied and extensive range of interests and activities, is reflected in the fact that Richard has a collection of nearly 100 different ties from the various clubs, organisations, and societies

to which he has belonged at one time or another over some fifty-
years, including: Playing Sport at club level: aged <30: lawn
tennis, and squash; aged >30: golf with a handicap ranging
between 17 and 20 at a number of clubs including: Strawberry
Hill, West Essex, Royal Automobile, Henley on Thames, and
Blankney; aged >60: croquet and bowls; Watching Football and
Cricket: season tickets over the years at: Nottingham Forest,
Chelsea, Arsenal, Reading, and Lincoln City; member of the
Marylebone Cricket Club (MCC) since 1989; Music: member of
the Glyndebourne Festival Society since 2007; Membership of
London Clubs: Royal Automobile Club, and Oriental Club;
Liveryman: granted the Freedom of the City of London in 1979;
Liveryman: Worshipful Company of Plumbers, 1986; Worshipful
Company of Wax Chandlers, 2007; Charitable: Knight
Commander of the Order of St. Lazarus of Jerusalem, CLJ in
1988, and promoted to KCLJ in 1990; Photography: remains a
long-standing hobby, the results of which decorate his home,
though it has to be added, restricted mostly to his study;
Community, a Presiding Magistrate for some eighteen years -
pro. bono., serving in: The City of London, Oxford, Nottingham,
and Lincoln, and on reaching the statutory retirement age in
2020, was placed on the Supplemental List, enabling him to
continue to be recognised as a Justice of the Peace and use the
letters J.P. after his name.

ND - #0010 - 200121 - C40 - 234/156/8 - PB - 9780853185901 - Gloss Lamination